RESTORE
CHANGING HOW YOU LIVE AND LOVE

STUDY GUIDE WITH LEADER'S NOTES

Robert K. Cheong

New
Growth
Press

newgrowthpress.com

New Growth Press, Greensboro, NC 27404
newgrowthpress.com
Cover Design: Faceout Books, faceoutstudio.com
Interior Design and Typesetting: Gretchen Logterman

ISBN: 978-1-64507-109-9 (Print)
ISBN: 978-1-64507-110-5 (eBook)

Printed in The United States of America

27 26 25 24 23 22 21 20   1 2 3 4 5

Contents

INTRODUCTION
THE REDEEMING POWER OF STORY

TO RESTORE is to give back something that was lost. Throughout the Scriptures, God restores position, power, land, and kingdoms. He restores comfort to the mourning and hope to the hopeless. To restore can also mean to mend something that is broken. The Scriptures describe God restoring the health, relationships, hearts, and souls of his people. God chooses an unexpected tool to make himself known and to show us how he restores. He uses stories.

During his time on earth, Jesus primarily communicated truth through stories. He didn't merely give moral instruction. Rather, Jesus spun tales about farmers and bankers and kings. Our Savior spoke about the sort of everyday realities with which his listeners could connect: growing crops, getting married, chasing lost sheep, and investing money. He did more than pass on knowledge. Jesus captivated the people's hearts and imaginations with mundane images that revealed eternal realities.

WHY STORY?

The journey of *Restore* helps you abide in the love of Christ in the midst of your realities, whether you are working through hard parts of your past, overwhelmed by life in the present, or seeking to grow as a disciple. *Restore* does this in a workbook format to help you interact with both your story and God's story through brief writing exercises. Ideally, you will first work through each *Restore* lesson on your own and then also discuss it in a small group, so that you can share your story and learn from the stories of others.

Stories aren't just for entertainment, and they aren't just fiction. Story is one of the most powerful and important truth-telling tools available. Here are a few reasons why:

- **God chose story.** Out of all the ways God could have revealed himself to us, he chose to share his story. The Bible contains many stories, and they add up to one big story—the story of who God is and what he has done for us.
- **Stories show us the big picture**. They give us a way to see our past, live in our present, and build hope for the future.
- **Stories build community.** They are meant to be told. When we tell our stories, we build a relationship with those who share and listen.

But God's story is different from all other stories. Beyond the fact that it is true beyond our imagination, *God's story is a story not only to be told, but a story to be lived.* God's story reveals the One who restores us despite the way evil has embedded brokenness, shame, and trauma into our story. God's story shows how he fulfills his promises to redeem every aspect of our story through his power and presence. And in the most personal and intimate way, God's story invites us to abide with Christ through both the dark valleys and the mountaintop experiences of life, and everything in between. Life, love, freedom, and joy are found only as we live with God in his story.

INTERSECTING STORIES

On the day Jesus rose from the dead, he joined two of his disciples as they traveled along a road. The two men tried to make sense of all that had happened over the past few days. They didn't recognize Jesus at first. So when he asked, "What are you discussing together as you walk along?" (Luke 24:17), they unpacked for him what had been consuming their thoughts—Jesus's crucifixion and reported resurrection.

Jesus began to travel with them. And as they moved along the road, Jesus shared how God's story, as told through the Old Testament Scriptures, pointed to him. Later, after Jesus departed, God's Spirit opened the disciples' eyes and they saw how the risen Savior personally connected God's big story with their own. Jesus's grand account moved them so deeply that they said, "Were not our hearts burning within us while he talked with us on the road and opened the Scriptures to us?" (Luke 24:32).

God wants you, like those travelers, to see that his story intersects with yours. God's story informs your story and gives meaning to your story. You see, our stories—like God's big story—are all about Jesus. And your story will find its ultimate meaning in light of his. He is the main character in a true tale about our redemption and restoration.

This journey you are about to begin will address your story's realities while helping you cling to the realities of God's story. At the intersection of God's story and your own, you will find that his love sustains you in your weariness, guides you in your confusion, and comforts you in your suffering. Moreover, the story of his love will compel you to live for him.

WHAT'S YOUR STORY?

As a first step, we must explore our own stories.

You may know your story well or you may not. You may have worked through big parts of your life story while other parts remain unexplored. God's timing for this is perfect. In his grace, God prepares us for when he would have us know and work through more of our stories.

Take Alexa, for instance. She was in her early thirties when God prompted her to begin to deal with the sexual abuse she had suffered as a teenager. Then in her late thirties, while standing in her kitchen, God helped her to see the connection between her "need" for order in her home and the disorder she had endured during a chaotic childhood. It wasn't until her early forties that God gave her the courage and grace to reconcile a broken relationship with her mom.

The goal of *Restore* is not to work through all of your story at once. But you do need to explore the parts that have impacted how you relate to God and others and have shaped how you view life and love. By exploring your story, you will also get to see how God has been—and will continue to be—at work throughout your life. As you look back at your life, God wants you to see and experience more of him.

God isn't calling you to endless introspection, but he does invite you to face the aspects of your story that have kept you from knowing him and from being known by others. He's relentlessly at work to free you from bondage as he untwists that which has been tangled by your own sin, the sins of others, and the brokenness of this world.

MEET THE DIVINE AUTHOR

God knows every detail of your story. He knew every detail of your life before you were born. And he wants you to know him more fully *through* your story, not in spite of it.

God is the divine author of your story. This doesn't simply mean he has sovereign authority over your life in a way where you have no choice. Rather, God is creatively involved with your life, shaping it in an ongoing way. Here are a few things you should know about the author of your story:

- **He's the author of relationship.** God doesn't simply want to teach his people lessons so that they change their behavior. He wants to draw close to his people so that they know him and follow him.
- **He's the author of the details, the God of the small things.** God uses people, places, and things others may see as unimportant for his big purposes.
- **He turns endings into beginnings.** Just when you think it's over, God starts something brand new.

GOD'S GOAL: TO RESTORE YOUR SOUL AND REDEEM YOUR STORY

If you are distracted by the struggles and demands of life, God wants you to be swept up by his glory. He wants you to find rest and relief in him.

If you have put your hope in your circumstances changing, God asks you to find your hope in his unchanging love, even if your circumstances never change.

If you have denied the painful realities of your story, God invites you to face them with him, in the refuge of his strong arms and the comfort of his tender mercy.

If you are consumed by the wickedness, injustice, and sadness of your story, God wants you to shift your gaze toward Christ so you can see how your story is consumed and transformed by his big story of relentless, redeeming love.

God knows you and he cares for you. Your pain breaks his heart. Your hopes are important to him. He has plans to use every part of your story to draw you close to him. He wants to deepen your dependence upon him and to help you rejoice in his comfort. He wants you to be compelled by his love so that you no longer live for yourself but for him.

God wants you to see that he is with you *in your story* and that he cares for you and will change you *through your story.* After all, any story told by God is the kind that you'll want to share with others, a story of hope.

God is calling you to live like you've never lived before. He wants your life to be free from debilitating fear, life-robbing fantasy, suffocating shame, drowning guilt, destructive anger, and hopeless sorrow. As you step into your story, God will meet you there. As you explore the dark and even unknown crevasses of your life, he also wants you to experience the breadth, depth, height, and width of his love.

This may be the first time you have looked at your story in an intentional way. You may be overwhelmed when you think about diving into some parts of your life.

Be encouraged. Your story is not one more thing you have to get right. You do not need to figure everything out by the end of this journey. Relax, and pay attention to what God brings to your mind. Take in your story like you would a great movie or a good book. As you do, God will do a beautiful, transforming work in your heart and life.

You can be confident that God will **reframe** how you see and experience life, as well as how you see and experience him. Christ will **restore** your soul as you abide in his love and find rest in him. God will **redeem** your story as he takes what was meant for evil and uses it to free you to love him and to live for him. You will look back and see how God's story has engulfed your story as the darkness fades, the fears subside, the bondage is loosened, and the sorrow turns to joy. In ways unimaginable, as you look back at your story you may no longer wish you could rewrite the unexpected and unwanted parts, since you've seen how God has used every aspect of your story to draw you into his love and to grow you in Christ.

May the Lord bless your journey!

HOW TO USE THIS WORKBOOK

FORMING YOUR GROUP

This *Restore* study guide has been used primarily in group contexts—discipleship groups, weekly community groups, and weekly ministry groups—whether in a local church or on the mission field. You can go through this workbook on your own, but you will get the most out of this material if you share your reflections with someone else after each lesson. Processing out loud with others always brings insights or makes connections you missed when working through the material alone, so your journey will be enhanced if you choose to work through this workbook in a group setting. You always learn and grow so much more as you listen and interact with those in your group week in and week out, because God created us to experience life in community with one another.

If you choose to take this journey with others, plan to meet together for at least thirteen sessions. Each participant should have their own workbook and should work through each lesson on their own before the group meets. You have many options as to the group composition. God works in amazing ways in all different kinds of groups. Here are some things to consider as you pray about the makeup of your group.

- If you want your group to have the freedom to share the full range of struggles in detail, then you may consider having a **women's or men's group**. If you take this route, please remember that although *Restore* can be helpful to groups formed around a specific struggle (like grief, pornography, substance abuse, sexual abuse, divorce care, etc.) it is not written for issue-specific struggles. The drawback of using any material for specific struggles is that such an emphasis can lead to (1) over-identifying with the particular struggle, (2) thinking you need to be in such an issue-specific group in order to deal with the struggle, and (3) overlooking other equally important areas of your life where you are not trusting and following Christ. Granted, each struggle has its particular nuances, but the beauty of *Restore* is that God's story addresses *every* way we are impacted by and respond to evil. Whatever your struggle, abiding with Christ is always going to be the key not only to persevering through the troubles of life but flourishing by the power of his Spirit.

- If you choose to have a **mixed group** of women and men, be sensitive to the realities of both single and married people. Also be aware of unhelpful dynamics between men and women, such as gender stereotypes, cultural biases, flirting, or power dynamics that could pit men and women against each other. Be careful not to discuss explicit details of sexual sin or sexual abuse, so as not to bring about additional shame or discomfort.

- If you choose to have a **married couples' group**, you want to make sure you hear from both husband and wife during group discussions, so that one spouse doesn't dominate or talk for the other. Also encourage spouses to focus mainly on themselves versus focusing on the other with blame and bitterness. Whenever a wife or husband reflects on what God is showing them, ask, "Have you shared that with your spouse?" Such questions serve as a reminder that every couple needs to share their hearts with one another, and that as they do, they will grow in oneness. Give opportunities for the husband and wife to share with each other during the group time as needed. In the busyness of life, most couples don't take the time to share at the heart level. Also, many couples report they don't know how to share beyond superficial or routine matters.

WHAT TO EXPECT IN EACH LESSON

To prepare for your time in a small group setting, read through and reflect on the Big Idea, Look Back, Backstory, and Response Activities sections several days before your meeting. If you wait until the day of the meeting, you will not have the space or time to soak in the material and you may miss what God has for you. During each group session, you will spend approximately an hour and thirty minutes working through each lesson, sharing reflections and encouraging one another. The time allotments given within the lessons indicate the time you will spend on each activity during the group time. Here is what most lessons include:

Big Idea. This is an opening sentence that summarizes the main point of the lesson.

Look Back. (15 minutes) Each week the group starts with an invitation for participants to summarize how God enabled them to live differently, based on the previous week's lesson. This time provides an opportunity for people to celebrate how God has been at work in their lives and also serves as mutual accountability.

The Backstory. (20 minutes reading and reflecting alone and 10 minutes reading aloud in a group) As you read the backstory in advance of your group meeting, I encourage you to read slowly and prayerfully, underlining or highlighting words, phrases, or truths that stand out to you. Avoid the temptation to gloss over a sentence or skip over a Bible passage because you think you already know it. Remember that the Word of God is living and active, and God will use it in your life. When something captures your attention, take a moment to reflect on it and get a sense of how your heart responds. You might jot down such reflections in the margins. Notice how God is inviting you to draw near to him for refuge, hope, and love.

While in the group, I encourage you to read each backstory article aloud as a review for those who already completed the lesson or as a first-time exposure for those who haven't read the material. Reading the lesson aloud should take no more than ten minutes.

Response Activities. (15–30 minutes on your own and 20 minutes of discussion in small group) After each backstory, you will have the opportunity to respond to questions based on the material. Complete these activities before your group meeting. The questions are meant to increase your awareness of how your story has impacted your relationship with God and others and resulted in patterns of how you live and love. The questions will also help you connect the truths and themes of God's story with the themes and struggles in your story. Some people simply record their responses in the workbook while others take more time and write in a journal for extended reflection. Each week you will keep track of the ways God shepherds you and how you experience his love by using the storyboard in the back of the workbook. This will help you tell others of God's love and power in the weeks and months to come, as he restores your soul and redeems your story.

While in the group, take time to both share what God is showing you through his story and to also listen as others reflect and make connections between God's story and their own. God often encourages and speaks to you through the reflections of those around you.

Read and Abide. (15 minutes of personal reflection—to be completed during the group meeting—and 20 minutes of discussion in small group) The most meaningful part of each lesson is drawing near to God through a Scripture passage so that the Word of God does the work of God. This is a sweet opportunity to hear God's heart through his Word. In this section, you will (1) start by opening your heart to God, Then you will (2) note truths from the passage, (3) reflect on how your heart struggles to receive those truths, (4) see how God speaks directly to your story, struggles, and themes, and (5) sense how he is inviting you to trust and obey him so that you can love him and others.

Look Ahead. (5 minutes) Each person will share how they will seek to live differently during the coming week based on God's invitation from the Read and Abide time.

Prayer. (5 minutes) Close out your time responding to God through prayer, giving him thanks for his faithfulness and love that you have experienced during the lesson and small group time. Ask for his Spirit to empower you to put into practice what he is teaching you so you can live and love differently.

SPIRIT-DEPENDENT GOALS

Though God will use this material to address the struggles in your life, don't approach this workbook as a self-help resource. Also avoid the temptation to complete this material simply to gain more academic information or to fill a discipleship checklist. Rather, approach each lesson as an opportunity to abide in the love of Christ as you receive, pray, and live his Word in the midst of your story.

Take a moment to read through these Spirit-dependent goals. Prayerfully mark each goal that you long for God to bring about in your heart and life.

Reconnect with God and find rest in him.

Truly my soul finds rest in God;
  my salvation comes from him.
Truly he is my rock and my salvation;
  he is my fortress, I will never be shaken. (Psalm 62:1–2)

Remember where your help and hope come from.

I lift up my eyes to the mountains—
  where does my help come from?
My help comes from the LORD,
  the Maker of heaven and earth. (Psalm 121:1–2)

Reframe how you see your story and struggles as you see God's story.

For our struggle is not against flesh and blood, but against the rulers, against the authorities, against the powers of this dark world and against the spiritual forces of evil in the heavenly realms. (Ephesians 6:12)

Restore your soul as you receive comfort from God and experience his love.

> The LORD is my shepherd; I shall not want.
>   He makes me lie down in green pastures.
> He leads me beside still waters.
>   He restores my soul. (Psalm 23:1–3 ESV)

> Praise be to the God and Father of our Lord Jesus Christ, the
> Father of compassion and the God of all comfort, who comforts
> us in all our troubles, so that we can comfort those in any trouble
> with the comfort we ourselves receive from God. (2 Corinthians
> 1:3–4)

Regain confidence in God.

> Now faith is confidence in what we hope for and assurance
> about what we do not see. (Hebrews 11:1)

> Praise the LORD!
> How joyful are those who fear the LORD
>   and delight in obeying his commands….
> Such people will not be overcome by evil.
>   Those who are righteous will be long remembered.
> They do not fear bad news;
>   they confidently trust the Lord to care for them. (Psalm 112:1,
>   6–7 NLT)

Reignite your love for God and others.

> Jesus replied, "'You must love the LORD your God with all your
> heart, all your soul, and all your mind.' This is the first and
> greatest commandment. A second is equally important: 'Love
> your neighbor as yourself.' The entire law and all the demands
> of the prophets are based on these two commandments."
> (Matthew 22:37–40 NLT)

How many of these goals do you think God will accomplish during your time going through *Restore*? Believe it or not, God delights in making each of these goals a reality every day as you live life with him in Christ.

LESSON 1
REFRAMING OUR REALITY
THROUGH THE LENS OF THE FALL

BIG IDEA

To understand your reality, you need to understand the common struggles that are a part of life in this world due to sin.

LOOK BACK (15 minutes)

Before you begin your journey through *Restore*, it may be helpful to take some time to see how you are doing. Many people are surprised, when they look back after *Restore*, to see the many ways God worked in their lives. Spend a few minutes in prayer and ask God to show you what he wants you to see and understand during this journey. Psalm 62:8 reminds us that God is our refuge and we can pour out our hearts to him.

What reality is most pressing, persistent, or painful? Take a moment and consider what occupies your heart and mind. You may find yourself circling back to something in the past, preoccupied with something in the present, or concerned about something in the future. Write down what comes to mind.

What is going on in your heart and soul? You can answer this by capturing your thoughts, emotions, and desires connected with your reality.

- My thoughts (What do I keep thinking about or what I keeps me up at night?)

- My emotions (What am I feeling or experiencing in my heart and soul?)

- My desires (What am I wanting or longing for?)

What's going on in your body? Your reality impacts both your body and soul. You may find that your breathing, sleeping, eating, tension, headaches, blood pressure, etc. are impacted by what's going on in your reality.

How does your reality impact your relationship with others? You may find yourself withdrawing from or blaming others. You may be struggling to trust, love, and forgive others.

How does your reality impact your relationship with God? God may seem distant. You may be in a dry season as you struggle to love, trust, and obey God.

What do you hope to experience or achieve through *Restore?*

THE BACKSTORY TO OUR COMMON STRUGGLES (10 minutes—Read aloud in group.)

Life is hard. Work can feel demanding and unsatisfying. Family life can be exhausting. Raising kids takes everything we have to offer. Money seems tight. Nurturing a marriage doesn't come naturally. Friends and family members fail us and wrong us. Our trying circumstances and troubling relationships make life a struggle. It's no coincidence that Paul describes our life as a "fight of the faith" (1 Timothy 6:12).

To complicate matters, your story and your struggles are unique. You have individualized DNA. Your life can't be lived by anyone else. Only you have experienced—and only you can relive—the pain and darkness of your unique story.

On the other hand, your story also is common. Like every human person, you are made in God's image, and you are living in God's story. Believe it or not, you experience struggles common to every person. Even the temptations you face are not unique. Others experience them too. Paul reminds us, "No temptation has overtaken you except what is common" (1 Corinthians 10:13).

Our Common Struggles are Rooted in Humanity's First Sin

God's story—and in particular the portion of God's story from Genesis 3 that you will read about below—will help you reframe how you see and experience your particular difficulties. You will become more aware of your heart and soul's common struggles, and you'll begin to relax as you discover that all people struggle in similar ways, realizing perhaps for the first time that you are not alone.

Later in *Restore*, you will explore the story we refer to as *the fall* in greater detail, but for now remember that the fall occurred when the first man and woman brought sin into the world by choosing not to trust and obey God. From that moment on, all humanity has dealt with some common struggles. Common struggles simply describe the ways we respond to evil as we live in a fallen world. Such struggles are not merely a passive response, but can also be an active response flowing from our thoughts, emotions, and desires. God created us to relate and respond to the people and circumstances around us.

Let's take a look at how these common struggles emerged around Adam and Eve's rebellion against God. As we walk through the account of the fall, keep one eye on Adam and Eve, and the other eye on how you can see such struggles in your own life.

Common Struggles Seen in the Story of the Fall

God created the first man and woman and gave them total freedom to live an abundant life in his presence and to enjoy all of his provisions in the garden of Eden. God told them only one thing that they could not do. But we know what happened next.

Fantasy (Genesis 3:1–6). Satan, disguised as a serpent, tempted Adam and Eve to envision a life in which they could be like God and didn't have to obey God's word. The serpent deceived Adam and Eve. He tricked them into thinking that when God commanded them not to eat from the tree of the knowledge of good and evil, he was keeping them from a better life. They fantasized about goodness and wisdom in ways contrary to God and his word. **Fantasy is refusing to accept or address your actual situation, instead seeking a different reality that offers an imagined escape or hope.**

Guilt (v. 7). As soon as Adam and Eve rejected God and his command by eating the forbidden fruit, they stood guilty before him. They had rejected God's word and disobeyed his will. **Guilt is pain that comes from something you've done wrong.**

Shame (v. 7). Adam and Eve also sensed something was wrong with themselves. They experienced shame and embarrassment over their sinfulness. **Shame is pain that comes from who you are or who you think you are.**

Fear (vv. 8–10). Adam and Eve soon heard God walking in the garden. God called out, "Where are you?" How did they respond? Instead of drawing near to God as they were created to do, they hid from him because they were afraid. **Fear is an anxious anticipation of something perceived to be threatening or dangerous.** Because of their guilt before God, Adam and Eve perceived their loving Creator as a threat to their lives.

Anger (vv. 11–13). When God asked the first man and woman what was going on, they responded with blame and bitterness: "The woman *you* gave me made me do it." **Anger is a strong feeling of displeasure or hostility in response to someone or something that opposes what you value.** Anger flows when we are displeased with people (God, self, others) or our life circumstances. Adam and Eve lashed out when God pursued them, blaming God and each other for their own sin.

Sorrow (vv. 16–24). Adam and Eve felt sorrow because of their guilt and shame before God and also because God judged them. They felt sorrow particularly when they were banished from the garden. **Sorrow is a deep sadness or despair, usually resulting from loss.** As the consequence of their sinful choices, Adam and Eve were no longer allowed to dwell in God's presence. This was an incredible loss.

Common struggles should not be understood as core sins. Jesus himself experienced some of the common struggles in his life on earth, and he is sinless. But common struggles become sinful when they drive how we live more than faith, and when they result in self-preoccupation rather than in loving God and others. Common struggles become sinful when they loom larger than God and lead us to live in ways contrary to how God created us to live.

Common Struggles Coexist and Comingle

It's important to understand how the common struggles play out in your heart and soul. Consider an iceberg. What you see above the surface of the water is only a small portion of what is actually there. In a similar way, the difficulties you face in your daily life can be an extension of the common struggles beneath the surface. When your common struggles dominate your life, they can wreak havoc in your heart and soul, impacting your relationship with God and others.

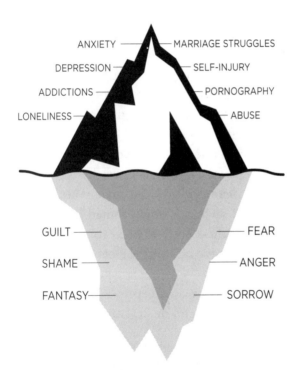

It's also important to know that the common struggles don't work alone or result in only one particular life challenge. We can't draw a straight line from fear to anxiety or from anger to abuse. Instead, various struggles combine and build upon one another to produce one or more issues.

We can think of the common struggles like the primary colors. You can create any shade of color from various combinations of red, blue, and yellow. In a similar way, your life troubles may be rooted in a combination of the common struggles. For instance, your sorrow and shame may yield loneliness, depression, and addiction. A couple's marriage issues may be driven primarily by one spouse's fantasy and anger and the other spouse's shame and fear.

Common Struggles Lead to Relational Struggles

These common struggles can overwhelm your soul and impact the way you relate to God and others. Consider some of your possible **relational struggles**:

- A struggle with **fantasy** can fuel discontentment with your spouse. It can drive you to escape reality and your responsibilities through some form of distraction or your drug of choice.
- A struggle with **guilt** can paralyze you with regret. Fixating on what you could have done differently or beating yourself up for not knowing better can rob you of joy.
- A struggle with **shame** can cause you to withdraw from God and others out of a sense that you are unworthy, inadequate, or a failure.
- A struggle with **fear** can leave you anxious and paranoid. You may be frightened of saying or doing something wrong. You may be afraid of letting others know the real you.
- A struggle with **anger** can hurt the people you love. Anger keeps others at a distance.
- A struggle with **sorrow** can keep you living in the past, keep you from enjoying the present, or steal any desire to live in the future.

The common struggles can lead to relational brokenness. Though this is the case, the very fact that these struggles are common to humanity should give us hope. The common struggles do not take God by surprise. As the sage said, "Everything that happens has happened before; nothing is new, nothing under the sun" (Ecclesiastes 1:9 CEV). God's story addresses all of the common struggles. When you face fantasy, shame, fear, guilt, anger, and sorrow, you can know that you are not alone. God knows your troubles. He is with you in them, and he has a plan to use them to make you more like Christ. Most importantly, God has given you his Son to be your refuge and hope in the midst of all these struggles.

RESPONSE ACTIVITIES (20 minutes)

Here is a selection of response questions and activities designed to stir your heart and soul and get you thinking deeply about the truths presented in this lesson. Write out your answers and reflections ahead of the group meeting, then be prepared to discuss your reflections together.

1. Which of the common struggles do you see in your heart and life? Mark all that apply on the checklist below. Don't be surprised if you see more than one struggle present.

   - ❏ **Fantasy.** You may struggle with discontentment and placing your hope in the "next thing." You may avoid conflict or painful situations, dream of different ways that life can be better, or seek to escape reality through work, video games, hobbies, drinking, or drugs.
   - ❏ **Guilt.** You may struggle with a sense of regret—that you should or could have done things differently. You may struggle to forgive yourself for what you have done. You may also wrestle with thinking that you can't do anything right or that you are always messing up and making the wrong choices.
   - ❏ **Shame.** You may feel different from everyone else. You may struggle with the sense that you'll never be good enough, that you have no worth or value. You may feel unloved or may think you don't deserve to be loved.
   - ❏ **Fear.** You may fear that God is not pleased with you. You may think you need to earn his love or believe he will condemn you in spite of the fact that you've trusted Christ. You may be afraid of what others think about you, worried that if they knew the real you, they would reject you. You may find yourself filled with anxiety or worry, constantly obsessing over worst-case scenarios.

❒ **Anger.** You may be filled with bitterness toward those who have wronged you, forgotten you, or who didn't meet your expectations. You may find yourself judging and blaming others. You may be cynical or sarcastic towards others—even God—because life has not turned out the way you envisioned or hoped.

❒ **Sorrow.** You may be sinking into despair. You are convinced that your circumstances will never change. You may become hopeless, thinking God does not care about you. Maybe you think your unanswered prayers prove that God doesn't care about you. You may be filled with regret as you reflect on what will never be or what should have been. Your grief can be overwhelming as you face the loss of a loved one or of a beloved dream.

Don't be overwhelmed if you identify with many or even all of these common struggles. Most people find themselves in the same position. You are not alone.

2. Write out some of the particular difficulties you face in your daily life right now. Are you able to see them as an extension of the common struggles?

3. As you consider how your troubles may be rooted in the common struggles we all face as a result of humanity's first sin, do you feel more anxious or more relieved? Jot down some thoughts that come to mind, or write out a prayer to God.

4. Storyboard: Take a moment to reflect, and then record a brief summary of what God is teaching you through this lesson. Record it at the start of your storyboard, which you can find beginning on page 183. The storyboard will let you capture how God is at work in you through each lesson. You will be able to see the subtle yet significant ways God is redeeming your story over the course of your *Restore* journey.

READ AND ABIDE: GENESIS 3
(15 minutes of personal reflection, followed by 20 minutes of group discussion)

This is where you draw near to God through his Word. In each lesson's Read and Abide section, you will read a Bible passage and reflect on what God says is true. Your purpose is to look beyond your struggles that loom large so that you see and believe God's bigger reality and follow him.

1. **Understand your reality.** Before you open the Word of God, open your heart to God. Which of life's common struggles feels most overwhelming or painful to you in your life right now?

2. **Look up and see God's reality.** Read **Genesis 3** slowly one or two times. This passage tells much about our sin and struggles. But how does Genesis 3 also show God's continuing love and care for you, or his plan to rescue you from sin and sorrow? Note any verses that stand out to you. (For example: "Verse 9—In my sin, God reaches out and comes to me.")

3. **Understand your heart struggles.** How do you, like Adam and Eve, find it easy to focus on yourself and your struggles and hard to have faith in God's goodness? What way of thinking that they needed to change do you also want to change?

4. **Abide and rest in God.** How does God's bigger plan for Adam and Eve, or his care for them, speak to your heart amid your struggles?

5. Follow God's invitation. How is God calling you to love him and others better right now because you can see beyond your struggles? (For ideas, refer back to the lesson's list of **relational struggles** on page 22.)

LOOK AHEAD (5 minutes)

List 1–2 practical ways you will seek to live differently this week based on God's invitation. Share your ideas with the group.

PRAYER (5 minutes)

Close out your time responding to God through prayer, giving him thanks for his faithfulness and love that you have experienced during the lesson and small group time. Ask for his Spirit to empower you to put into practice what he is teaching you so you can live and love differently.

IMPORTANT NOTE: As you look ahead to lesson 2, plan to get started on it early. Lesson 2 will ask you to think about your personal story. Ideally, this lesson is most helpful when you take time to reflect on it over several days or even a full week.

LESSON 2
FACING YOUR REALITY
THROUGH YOUR STORY

BIG IDEA

Your story helps you see how your experiences have shaped the way you see life, understand yourself, and relate to God and others.

IMPORTANT NOTE: This lesson is structured differently from the others. Please plan to complete all activities through Step 6 on your own ahead of the group meeting.

THE BACKSTORY ON YOUR STORY

You experience reality through your story. The story you live—whether it's about some past experience, present struggle, or future unknown—can become your frame of reference. When it does, it influences how you see, experience, and respond to life. Your story may revolve around only you, or it may include someone else such as a parent, friend, spouse, or child.

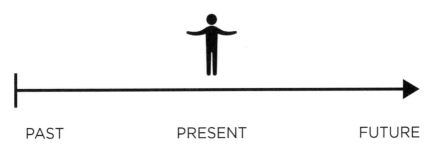

PAST   PRESENT   FUTURE

This lesson will guide you through the process of understanding your story. The lesson is divided into three sections—**remember, reflect, and recap.** It involves (1) recording significant experiences from your life and (2) identifying themes in those experiences as well as in your responses to those experiences so that, (3) when you finish, you will have a short, insightful version of a slice of your life story that is ready to share with others.

Before completing this activity or answering any questions, read through the entire lesson. This will allow you to see the big picture before you begin. Then, you can work through each step in a reflective way, allowing God the space to help you consider what comes to mind. Feel free to make multiple passes at a particular step if you find the need. You may complete the entire process in one sitting or break up the steps as your schedule or ability to remember and reflect allows. The activities provided in this lesson are essential for you to prepare your story to share with others.

Some people spend 2–3 hours reflecting, praying, and writing out a portion of their story. Others might set aside a week, knowing that they do better with extended time to reflect and pray, stop for needed time and space, then resume hours or a day later. Some write things out, then process with a friend, family member, or spouse. Whatever approach you take, please know that the time and effort you take to prepare will lay the foundation for the rest of your time in *Restore.*

REMEMBER

Step 1: Pray

As you begin, set aside a few minutes for prayer. Ask God to show you the areas of your life he wants you to understand more fully. He may be prompting you to reflect on a particular part of your story in a new way. There may even be parts of your story you've been unwilling to face that he is inviting you to process for the first time.

This is a good time to acknowledge that working through some aspects of your story could bring up strong emotions, even anxiety or panic. Bring such concerns to the Lord in prayer. Ask him to give you peace when you feel overwhelmed or when you're tempted to distance yourself from him or from others.

ELAINE'S EXPERIENCE: When Elaine started to work through her story, she knew that thinking about her child's chronic illness would be extremely difficult. Thinking about this situation had always been painful and confusing. Talking about it had always seemed to make it worse. When faced with the prospect of sharing this part of her story, a sense of fear and anxiety mounted against her like waves. Elaine felt like she was drowning. Then, God brought to her mind a prayer from Psalm 61:2–3, "Lead me to the rock that is higher than I. For you have been my refuge." She felt the Lord's comfort lift her up. When she told her story, Elaine still felt waves of painful emotions, but she held on to the promise that God is her refuge, and she grew to hope in his work in her life.

Step 2: Write out some of your life experiences.

Grab a journal, your laptop, or some sheets of paper as you work through the following steps.

Take some time to reflect and remember some events from your life, good or bad, that have impacted you. The experiences you record may range from big moments to small interactions. Don't let anything be off limits. If you feel stuck, use some of the questions below to stir your memory.

- Are there **desires or thoughts** that come up in the quiet moments of your day? Consider those moments, and work backwards. Have you experienced similar desires or thoughts in the past? How might these thoughts or desires connect with a past experience or difficult relationship?
- Do you have **relationships that feel strained** or that you would describe as broken? What led to the relational struggles?

- Which **people** have had the greatest influence on your life, positive or negative? How so?
- What **events** or moments mark turning points in your life? What came before and after these moments?
- How do you **see yourself**? How do you want others to see you? What motivates you? What is important for others to know about you? There may be some events or experiences that have shaped how you see yourself, fuel your motivation, or drive how you want others to see you.
- What **hardship or suffering** have you faced? Thinking back to how you grew up, how did you learn to deal with conflict or disappointment?
- What are some moments of great **joy** that have impacted you? What brings you joy and pleasure?
- If you're married, be sure to jot down some life-shaping experiences both from **before and during your marriage**. Focus on understanding your own heart and your own part in the themes and patterns of your marriage. Don't direct your energy toward blaming or changing your spouse. Specifically, what are the significant moments in your marriage? Where do you see subtle drifts in direction or sharp turns?
- What **religious experiences** have shaped you, positively or negatively? Did you grow up believing something different than you do now? When have you felt closest to God? When did you feel most distant? What are some moments that have shaped how you view God?
- What **ministry experiences** have been particularly hard or painful? How has this experience impacted how you see the church and relate to God's people? Focus on understanding your own heart and your own part in the themes and patterns of the ministry experiences. Don't direct your energy toward blaming or changing others. Specifically, what are the significant moments in your years of ministry? Where do you see subtle drifts in direction or sharp turns?

Step 3: Arrange your life experiences in chronological order.

After writing down your experiences, organize them within the three major phases of life:

1. Childhood
2. Youth
3. Adulthood

New experiences may come to mind as you complete this step. Take time to consider which have had the greatest influence and which stages of life brought the most impact.

REFLECT

Step 4: Examine one life experience at a time.

Use a simple chart like the ones that follow to help you organize your thoughts and feelings around some of the most significant or life-shaping events. Choose one or more of the experiences from step 2 that you'd like to work through and examine on a deeper level. Then, use the chart to highlight its impact.

In the first row, write down a particular **life experience**. This may be a single event or a season of your life.

In the second row, write down words or phrases that describe the **theme** you associate with that experience. At its most basic level, a theme is just a big idea. It's the underlying message you received from that experience. For example, when you tell about the time your dad planned a fishing trip for just the two of you, the events of the day make up the story and the theme of that story is the message you took from it. In this case, your dad had to call off the anticipated fishing trip because of work. As a result, you received a message of not feeling loved and experienced the effects of broken promises. So you could write "not loved" or "broken promises" as the themes.

In the third row, consider how this particular life experience has **impacted** your relationship with God, yourself, and others, paying special attention to the negative impacts. (Your themes should not be limited to the common struggles.)

Example 1: Reflection on a Life Experience

Life experience	Parent's divorce		
Themes	Loneliness	Distrust	Inadequacy
Impact on my relationships with God, self, and others	**Others** — No one loves me. **God** — Where was God when my family fell apart? Does he really love me?	**Others** — My parents said they loved each other and me. I can't trust anyone! **God** — I can't trust him.	**Self** — I'm not good enough to keep my family together. **God** — Even God couldn't keep my parents together.

Life experience			
Themes			
Impact on my relationships with God, self, and others			

Example 2: Reflection on a Life Experience in Marriage

Life experience	Our marriage conflicts		
Themes/patterns	Shame	Harshness	Name-Calling
Impact on my relationships with God, self, and spouse	**Spouse** — I will never be good enough for my spouse. **God** — Does God even love me?	**Spouse** — I feel like I walk on eggshells given the constant critique. **God** — Why doesn't God change my spouse?	**Self** — I have no voice in my marriage and feel humiliated. **God** — God doesn't want me to be happy. How long do I have to stay married?

Life experience			
Themes or patterns			
Impact on my relationships with God, self, and spouse			

Rather than a particular event or season, you may feel led to reflect on an impactful relationship such as one with a family member. You are impacted most by those who are closest to you. Your family members' presence or absence, their love or neglect, can have a profound effect on the way you view reality.

ERIC'S EXPERIENCE: When Eric listed his life experiences, he quickly noticed that most of the hurtful times he'd recorded involved his mother. But his mother was also there for many of his joyful times. He decided he wanted to focus on his relationship with his mom, so he added some of these instances where she had hurt him, as well as how she had become more supportive as he got older.

If you've found a similar pattern in your life experiences, simply place the name of the impactful person in the first row of your chart and combine experiences and themes in the second row. Write out as many experiences and themes related to this relationship as God brings to mind.

Example 3: Reflection on an Impactful Relationship

Family member	Mom		
Experiences And themes	Forgot to pick me up at school, forgot my recitals **Others** — No one remembers my birthday.	Harsh discipline, yelling and name calling	Change. Mom became more loving when I was in high school.
Impact on my relationships with God, self, and others	**Others** — No one remembers my birthday. **Self** — I am not worth remembering, not valued.	**God** — I always feel I have to be obedient to God or else he will punish me. I try hard to please God, but feel like I never measure up.	**God** — He can change anyone. **Self** — My mom changed but I didn't. What's wrong with me?

Family member			
Experiences And themes			
Impact on my relationships with God, self, and others			

Step 5: Look back over your experiences to discover larger themes and patterns.

After charting out your experiences and relationships, take time to reflect on what has come to light. When you look over the events that have had significant impact upon you, you may be able to connect the dots between your life experiences. Maybe several of your major experiences involve loss or betrayal. Perhaps they taught you that your performance or success is the most important thing about you. Or maybe a theme may surface of needing control or being controlled.

Answer one or more of the following questions below to spark your thinking about larger themes and patterns in your story.

- Which experiences, relationships, or themes have had the biggest impact on (1) how you view yourself, (2) how you relate to others, or (3) how you relate to God? Explain why.

- God put you in your family. How do you react to that statement? What questions does it raise in your mind?

- What triggers a negative response in you? Are there looks you receive that spark shame? Do particular tones of voice ignite fear? Is there a certain touch that triggers a sense of dread? What negative memories from your past may be the root of these triggers?

- As you've thought back through your life experiences, has a larger theme or pattern emerged? How does that pattern of experiences impact how you live and how you love others in the present?

Here are some questions to help you think more deeply about your **life patterns** (how you tend to respond to life). You can capture your reflections on the My Story Summary at the end of the lesson (page 41).

Do you tend to do depend mainly on yourself, thinking you can't trust or depend upon others?

- Have you developed a cynical or pessimistic view of life?
- Do you tend toward despair or joy?
- How do you respond to negative circumstances?
- Do you tend to isolate yourself or shut down when you are overwhelmed?
- Do you tend to escape through entertainment, food, drink, or drugs to help you to cope with life?
- Do you tend to do things your own way or do you look to God and others for counsel?

Here are some questions to help you think more deeply about your **relational patterns** (how you tend to respond to God and others). You can capture your reflections on the My Story Summary at the end of the lesson.

- Do you struggle with trusting others or God?
- Do you avoid working through conflict?
- When you receive feedback, do you feel insecure or get defensive?

- Do you forgive quickly and move on, or do you hold onto bitterness?
- Do you tend to want boundaries to protect yourself from more hurt? Does God's love seem absent or beyond reach?

RECAP

Step 6. Write your story.

Now that you've reflected on your experiences, themes from your past, and their impact on your relationships, select a piece of your story that you want to focus on and write it out in your journal. You can be creative in the way you do this:

- You might write out the story as though you are telling it to a friend then read it aloud.
- You could write your story as though you are a reporter, writing an article on "The Story of (Your Name)"
- You could draw a timeline and label it with life events in one color and themes in another.
- You could tell your story out loud, record it, and then listen to it.
- You may even outline your story, using bullets, numbers, and sub-points to organize the information you've gleaned through this lesson.

You can't address everything at once, so don't include your entire life story. First, pray and ask God to show you which aspects of your story he wants you to concentrate upon at this time. Then, look back at the memories and themes you've explored during this exercise and choose one or two experiences that have had the greatest impact on your life that you either haven't processed or would like to work through again. Even if you have addressed a particular experience before, God may continue to restore your soul and redeem your story in ways you may not expect.

After preparing your story, summarize the themes, struggles, life patterns, and relational patterns (patterns of loving) on the My Story Summary worksheet on the next page.

You should also write down the themes on your storyboard at the back of this book (page 183). Remember, the storyboard will keep track of how God *reframes* how you see and understand your life, how he *restores* your soul, and how he *redeems* your story as you journey through each lesson.

Step 7: Share your story. (10 minutes per person)

A story doesn't reach completion until it's shared. If you are working through this workbook alone, be sure to ask a friend, family member, or your spouse if you can share your story with them.

If you are journeying with others, you will share your story in your group. Everyone in the group will have a chance to tell their stories and to listen to others. Though you will have only a brief time to share your story, know that you'll be able to share and talk more about your struggles and your story's themes during the following weeks.

Please know there are no right or wrong parts of your story to share. The main thing to remember is to share the slice of your story that God is inviting you to share so that he can redeem that part of your story and he can restore your soul.

You will have ten minutes to share your story. Though this is a brief time, you will be surprised how much of your story you can share in ten minutes, particularly when you prepare ahead of time. Be sure to prepare well by working through the Remember and Reflect sections above so that you are able to share your story in a clear and concise way. It usually helps to begin by sharing your theme or themes, then share relevant parts of your story in a chronological way that highlights your themes.

If you are married, but your spouse is not going through *Restore* with you, we encourage you to invite your spouse to work through lesson 2 with you so that you can both benefit from this exercise.

If you are in a married couples' group, the format and timing for sharing your story will be slightly different. Each couple will have twenty minutes to share. Each spouse should take five minutes to share their story, themes, and patterns from before marriage. Then, the couple will have ten minutes to share together about agreed-upon themes and patterns within their marriage. Couples should share aspects of marriage they can celebrate as well as what they want to work through during *Restore*.

MY STORY SUMMARY

Jot down the main takeaways from your story so you can use this page for a quick reference as you work through God's story. Summarize the themes, struggles, significant life experiences, life patterns, and relational patterns below.

Themes and common struggles:

Significant life experiences that relate to these themes:

Life patterns (how I tend to respond to life):

Relational patterns (how I tend to respond to God and others):

SMALL GROUP GUIDELINES

Here are some helpful practices to follow when sharing or caring for others in your small group. Most apply not only to this lesson, but are helpful in any group sharing time.

When Sharing Your Story

1. **Focus on yourself.** Don't offer general reflections: "we tend to do this" or "others tend to do that." Rather, speak in terms of "I" or "me" as you offer personal reflections. Also, don't focus on or talk about other people in your story to blame them or to change them. If you are married, you are encouraged to share how you desire to grow in loving your spouse.
2. **Share a slice of your story.** Share the slice that is most painful, pressing, or persistent. Limit what you share so others can share, too. Do not simply share your conversion testimony. If you work in vocational ministry, do not simply share your call to ministry.
3. **Start with the theme(s).** Start with the theme(s) you've identified and share the aspects of your story that support the theme(s).
4. **Watch your time.** You will have ten minutes to share your story. Couples will have twenty minutes.
5. **Remember God's sovereign care.** God already knows your story and will redeem every aspect of it as you journey through life with him.

Listening to Someone Who Shares

1. **Look at the person sharing.** This communicates that you are listening and that you care. Watch for body language such as tears or the person's posture. We communicate with more than just our words. Also, do not eat or look at your phone when people are sharing.
2. **Listen with love.** Have a loving curiosity. Listen with your heart, and listen to their heart—their thoughts, emotions, and desires (TED). Be aware of your own nonverbal reactions when you hear difficult details. On the one hand, ensure that your face reflects your loving heart. On the other hand, make sure your face doesn't

reflect any judgment or disgust that you may have in your heart (pray for God to remind you of the grace and forgiveness he has given you in Christ).

3. **Love the person sharing.** The person will sense your love as you look and listen with grace and compassion. Respect the confidentiality of what you hear. This is not your story to share.

Responding to Someone Who Shares

The initial moments after someone shares can be filled with a sense of shame and fear. The person who shares may feel exposed and vulnerable. Follow these guidelines:

1. **Don't ask questions.** Immediately after someone shares is not the time to ask questions unless there is the possibility of harm to self or others.

2. **Say thank you.** Thank the person for sharing, for being courageous in their vulnerability, and for entrusting their heart to you and others in your group.

3. **Express sorrow and acknowledge their pain.** For example, you might say, "My heart aches for all that you went through."

4. **Encourage but don't affirm.**[1] You can encourage a person by referencing specific ways they are trusting Christ in the midst of their suffering. For example, you might say, "I was encouraged by what you shared, because I hear a person who is clinging to Jesus" or "As you shared, I could see how God was giving you strength and courage." Encouragement is centered on Christ and seeks to reassure the person in Christ. Affirming the other person, by contrast, is merely trying to help them feel better about themselves. Don't say, for example, "You *are* a good person" or "You can do it! You are smart. You are strong." Affirmation is centered on the person and seeks to reassure them about themselves. Affirming others in this way can add more weight to their weariness.

5. **Encourage as a community.** After a person shares, everyone in the group can share what encouraged them while they were listening.

God uses such communal encouragement to grow and bless everyone.

6. **Don't do the following:**
   - Assume you can understand: "I know how you feel."
   - Turn the attention back on yourself: "That happened to me."
   - Offer solutions: "Let me tell you what worked for me."

After each person or couple shares, the group will encourage and then pray for them.

TIPS FOR THE WEEKS AFTER YOU SHARE YOUR STORIES

1. **Focus on God's story.** After every one has shared their stories, you will begin in the following weeks to work through God's story. Even though you will keep your story and themes in mind each week, you are encouraged to spend more time from this point forward focusing on God's story, especially seeing how the truths and themes in God's word address your reality and story.

2. **Learn from one another.** God works in and through his people. Listen carefully when others share a reflection or their experience with God. God can and will use what others share to help you connect the dots in your own story and to encourage your faith.

3. **Love one another.** Remember that God has you in *Restore* not only for yourself, but also for you to love those in your group. You can love others as you listen to them attentively, as you encourage them toward Christ, as you weep and rejoice with them, and as you share how you see Christ at work in them, especially given the details of their story.

4. **Keep the group in the loop.** You may feel the need to talk with your small group leader outside of the group time. If you do and the topic is appropriate to share, keep others up-to-date by giving a summary of the conversation to your group the following week so they can hear more about what you are wrestling with and how they can encourage and pray for you.

LESSON 3
KNOWING GOD AND HIS REALITY
THROUGH HIS STORY

BIG IDEA

God's bigger and brighter story is your story too, but the worries of this world make it hard to see.

LOOK BACK (15 minutes)

Discuss among your group how God has been at work in your heart and soul since you shared your story. Also share any spiritual warfare you may have experienced since last week.

THE BACKSTORY ON GOD'S STORY (10 minutes—Read aloud in group.)

It's easy for us to go through the day without any thought of God. Even as Christians, we can get so focused on our circumstances that we fixate on our worries and stresses. Those realities loom bigger than life.

Have you experienced days when you have been so stressed and overwhelmed that you feel you are about to explode? In those moments, perhaps you've gotten up to go outside because you just need some air. Then, as soon as the sun hits your skin, you look up. Your eyes lock upon the expansive blue sky and the patches of bellowing, white clouds. You smell the fresh spring air and notice a bee buzzing from flower to flower. Suddenly, your world opens up and you realize that life is so much bigger than the problem or person that weighed you down with anxiety.

We can get so fixated on our own narrow perspective that we forget there is a larger reality at play. We can forget that our individual stories are part of God's bigger story, the narrative of how he created us, personally pursued us, and rescued us from a life of sin and death so that we might live with him forever.

This lesson and the ones that follow will guide you through a process of understanding God's story. In this lesson, we will provide an overview of God's story. Like lesson 2, the backstory article is divided into three parts—remember, reflect, and recap. But before we turn to God's story, let's take a moment to look at the author.

God, the Author of His Story

You can more fully understand and appreciate a work of art if you know the artist's point of view, intentions, and even the backstory that inspired the piece, whether it be a painting, song, or novel. In the same way, in order to understand and appreciate God's story, we need to take a moment to get to know his backstory, perspective, and intentions.

Before he created the heavens and the earth, God existed and enjoyed a life of both love and glory. God exists as one God as three distinct, yet inseparable persons, sometimes called the Trinity—Father, Son, and Holy Spirit. They have always existed together, always worked together, and always enjoyed life together. When the Son, Jesus, prayed to the Father, he said, "You loved me before the creation of the world" (John 17:24)

As Father, God loves, gives life, and delights in his Son through his Spirit.[2] In fact, love originates with God because God is love. Since God is love, it is impossible for him not to love. Love always flows from the Father to the Son by his Spirit. We need to remember this progression of love since we can struggle to see God the Father as loving. Such a view may stem from teachings that portray God as an angry, judgmental, hard-to-please God who expects us to be perfect and punishes us when we are not. We can also be tempted to see God as unloving, absent, or abusive given how our own father or mother dealt with us.

The Son, who is the exact representation of the Father, radiates the Father's glory (Hebrews 1:3). The Son not only receives love from the Father, but also looks to him for word and deed. Jesus spoke only what he heard from the Father (John 12:49) and did only what he also saw the Father doing (John 5:19). Jesus said, "I have come down from heaven not to do my will but to do the will of him who sent me" (John 6:38). Jesus is the perfect "image of the invisible God" (Colossians 1:15).

The Holy Spirit is the third person of the Trinity. The Father shares his love with his Son through his Spirit. The Spirit of God empowered Jesus to do the will of the Father (Luke 4:1, John 1:32–34). The Spirit is like a conduit for the love and joy that flow back and forth between the Father and Son—"the fellowship of the Holy Spirit" (2 Corinthians 13:14). As we work through God's story, we will see how the Spirit works in us the same way he works in the Son.

Why did God create the heavens and earth if he already enjoyed a perfect life? God was not lonely. He was not seeking love. He was not lacking in glory. The simple answer is that God the Father wanted to share his love for his Son with others so that more people might experience and enjoy his love though an intimate relationship. In short, love inspired God to write a story that includes you and me.

Remember

There are four big movements of God's story—creation, fall, redemption, and consummation. At creation, we see how God created us for love. The fall shows us how evil keeps us from love. Redemption shows us how Jesus restores us with love. Consummation shows us how we will enjoy love forever.

Consider the following diagram. It shows how our stories, represented by the timeline at the bottom, are far more glorious than they appeared when we first looked at the timeline in our last lesson. Our stories actually are encompassed within God's bigger story, represented by the arc.

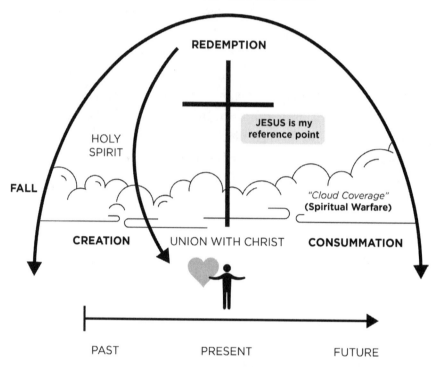

GOD'S REALITY
Revealed through God's Story of Love

REDEMPTION

JESUS is my reference point

HOLY SPIRIT

FALL

"Cloud Coverage" **(Spiritual Warfare)**

CREATION   UNION WITH CHRIST   **CONSUMMATION**

PAST   PRESENT   FUTURE

MY REALITY
My Story, My Struggles

My DEFAULT reference point

Our default way to view our stories is to see only below the clouds. Just as clouds sometimes cover up our view of the sun, Satan tries to blind us from seeing that our realities are part of God's larger reality. One spiritual warfare tactic of the Enemy's dark forces is to make us think our lives are confined to the things we can see in this world. Evil deceives us so that we feel like God is distant, and it tempts us to doubt his love. As a result, we tend to live "below the clouds."

Even on an overcast day, the sun is shining brightly above the clouds. Have you ever been at the airport on a dark, rainy day? When the plane takes off and punches through the clouds, what do you see through the window? You see the bright sun and blue skies. But if you look down, you still see the clouds. In the same way, God's glory and love are always present even when our reality looks to be filled with gloom and darkness.

The cross of Jesus, applied to you by the Holy Spirit, forever connects your story to God's bigger and brighter story. God now invites you to look up at Jesus and see through the clouds. God calls you to make Jesus your new reference point, and to see the story of his boundless love for you.

Reflect

In lesson 2, we learned that a theme is a big idea. It's the underlying message communicated through a string of experiences or events in a story. Some primary themes of God's story are **love** and **communion**.

God created the first man and woman in his image, to share his love. God created us to live in loving communion, or intimate fellowship, with God the Father, Son, and Holy Spirit. He made us for a relationship where we can personally know and experience God as Father, Son, and Holy Spirit. He made us to know and experience his love so that we can love him and others.

It didn't take long for the first man and woman to reject God's love. Adam and Eve disobeyed God's command when they ate the fruit of the knowledge of good and evil. As a result, their communion with God was broken. All men and women since have been born sinful and are driven by self-love rather than by God's love. God knew that people would be helpless against the power of sin and death, and he planned the perfect way to break the power of self-centered love.

While we were still his enemies, God showed his love for us by sending Jesus to save us from our sins and to bring us back into communion with him. It was the perfect rescue mission: the Father sent the Son from heaven to earth, and the Son took on a body and soul like ours. Jesus, being fully God and fully human, displayed God's love through his life of ministry and through his death on the cross. But Jesus was raised from the dead and ascended back to the Father so that those who repent and believe in him would be reconciled back into communion with God.

God gives new life to everyone who trusts in Jesus. He brings us into union with Christ—connecting our stories to his by raising us from death to life and by giving us the royal status of those who are seated in heaven with our risen Savior, whose lives are "now hidden with Christ in God" (Colossians 3:3). As we abide in the love of Christ, he restores our souls broken by sin.

At the end of time, when God establishes the new heavens and earth, our struggle against sin will finally be over and God's peace will rule forever. Jesus will be united in marriage to his bride, the church, and our communion with God will be perfect and we will enjoy his love forever. There will no longer be any need for the sun or moon, because God's glory will be our light, and we will spend eternity loving and being loved by God, as we love others.

Recap

Remember that a story doesn't reach completion until it's shared. Before you move ahead to the response activities below, find a friend or your spouse and retell them God's story in your own words.

RESPONSE ACTIVITIES (20 minutes)

Here is a selection of response questions and activities designed to stir your heart and soul and get you thinking deeply about the truths presented in this lesson. Write out your answers and reflections ahead of the group meeting, then be prepared to discuss your reflections together. **Consider your themes as you work through these questions.**

1. Describe your experience of life "below the clouds," when God seems distant and you struggle to know and experience his love.

2. Consider the themes of love and communion in God's story. Allow them to stir your imagination and heart. What it would look like for you to experience these realities in your everyday life?

3. Read the following reflections on God's character and then follow the instructions below.

> How can you know someone's character? You can listen to what they say, and you can watch what they do. But even then, you may know a person's public character but not know a different side they keep private, behind closed doors where only few can observe, or in the secret parts of their hearts. But when it comes to God, what you see is what you get. God does not lie (Numbers 23:19). He is the same publicly, privately, and even in secret. Why? Because God doesn't change. There is no variation or shifting shadow in his character (Psalm 102:27; Malachi 3:6; James 1:17). God also reveals his heart through his Word. We can also trust God because of his good works, which flow from his character.
>
> At the heart of God's character are the themes of his story. God is glorious and loving, and he desires to live in holy communion with his people. God satisfies our deepest longings, because he is love (1 John 4:8, 16), he is joy (Psalm 16:11; 21:6; John 15:11; 17:13), and he is peace (John 14:27; Romans 15:33; Philippians 4:7–9).
>
> In our troubles, God is our refuge, rock, and fortress (Psalm 46:1; 62:8). He is our strength (Psalm 46:1; 96:6). He is our hope (Romans 15:13; Hebrews 6:19–20; 1 Peter 1:3). He is our help (Psalm 121). He is our rest (Psalm 62:5; Matthew 11:28–30; Hebrews 4:10–11). He is the God of all comfort who comforts us in all of our troubles (Psalm 95:3–7; Isaiah 40:10–13; 2 Corinthians 1:3–4).

In our doubts, God is wisdom (1 Corinthians 1:24; Colossians 2:2–3). His name is Faithful and True (Revelation 19:11). He is the way, the truth, and the life (John 14:6).

Here are three additional aspects of God's character:

- First, he is **all-knowing** (1 John 3:20). He knows and directs the laws of the universe (Job 38:25–33). God knew every day of your life before you were born (Psalm 139:16). He also knows every thought, every emotion and desire, and everything we do or say (Psalm 139:1–4; John 2:24–25).

- God is also **all-present** (Jeremiah 23:23–24). He is everywhere all the time. God exists in the past, present, and future. God is not limited by time or space like us. The Bible says, "With the Lord, a day is like a thousand years, and a thousand years are like a day" (2 Peter 3:8). There is nowhere we can go to escape from his presence (Psalm 139:7–9).

- Finally, God is **all-powerful** (Revelation 1:8), meaning that he can do anything and everything he wills according to his purposes and plans (Psalm 115:3). His power is unlimited and unequaled (Ephesians 3:20). Nothing is too hard for God (Jeremiah 32:17).

You can trust God, knowing that he is true to his word, never changes, and is all-knowing, all-present, and all-powerful.

Write down one or more of God's character traits that you long to experience more deeply. Read and meditate on the verses in parentheses next to those attributes, and ask God to help you to know and experience these particular aspects of who he is.

4. Storyboard: Take a moment to reflect on the beauty of God's story, and then turn to page 183 and fill out your storyboard thoughts on this lesson.

READ AND ABIDE: PSALM 25
(15 minutes of personal reflection, followed by 20 minutes of group discussion)

1. **Understand your reality.** Open your heart to God before you open the Word of God. What recent, "below-the-clouds" stresses in your life have focused your attention away from him?

2. **Look up and see God's reality.** Read **Psalm 25** slowly one or two times. List the truths about God that stand out to you. Also, list some of the hard-to-see but real ways David asks God to care for him. Pick some that are especially meaningful to you. Why are they meaningful? Note any verses that stand out to you. (For example: "Verse 3—God, no one who hopes in you will be put to shame.")

3. **Understand your heart.** Verse 4 is a prayer to be able to see through the clouds: "Show me your ways, LORD, teach me your paths." What part of God's care do you struggle to really see and believe, even though you might read about it right here in this psalm? Write a one-sentence prayer asking God to teach it to you.

4. **Abide and rest in God.** How is the loving care David requests from God similar to the loving care you need? How is God assuring you that amid your stress he is your refuge?

5. **Follow God's invitation.** This entire psalm is a declaration of faith: "In you, LORD my God, I put my trust" (v. 1). How might your trust in God's loving care for you free you up to care lovingly for someone else? Try to think of a specific thing you might do.

LOOK AHEAD (5 minutes)

List 1–2 practical ways you will seek to live differently this week based on God's invitation. Share your ideas with the group.

PRAYER (5 minutes)

Close out your time responding to God through prayer, giving him thanks for his faithfulness and love that you have experienced during the lesson and small group time. Ask for his Spirit to empower you to put into practice what he is teaching you so you can live and love differently.

LESSON 4
CREATION:
GOD CREATED US FOR LOVE

BIG IDEA

God made you for a wonderful purpose: to know him deeply, to experience him intimately, and to reflect his goodness in all you do.

LOOK BACK (15 minutes)

Discuss among your group how God has enabled you to live differently, based on his invitation from the previous lesson's Read and Abide time.

THE BACKSTORY ON CREATION (10 minutes—Read aloud in group)

Think of your story as a suspense thriller or a gripping drama. In such stories, things initially appear one way but then take sudden turns as bits of truth come to light. When looking back or watching the movie a second time, we can now see what details were important. Now our eyes are open to what had been true all along. In a similar way, knowing the movements of God's story offers the necessary perspective to make sense of our own story. **God's story helps us to reframe, or reinterpret, our experiences so that we can understand and respond to our past and also live in the present differently.**

Now that we've walked through an overview of God's story and its major themes, we will examine each movement in God's story more closely. We can rest, knowing that God never minimizes or denies our story. Instead, God wants us to see how his story gives meaning, hope, and redemption to our story.

The Power and Wisdom of God's Word

God's story begins with creation. "He made the earth by his power; he founded the world by his wisdom and stretched out the heavens by his understanding" (Jeremiah 51:15). With just a word, our creator God stretched out billions of galaxies. With just a word, he designed sea creatures that live nearly seven miles below the ocean's surface. With just a word, he wrote into being the laws of nature and physics, which keep the earth both rotating on its axis and in orbit around the sun. With just a word, the creator God designed the anatomy and physiology of the human body. His matchless power, wisdom, and understanding crafted each person's thirty trillion cells. Like an artist with a blank canvas, he painted life and beauty where there was only a void. By his word, God created the universe out of nothing, "so that what is seen was not made out of what was visible" (Hebrews 11:3). Where there was only emptiness, God's word brought forth life.

God's Purpose for You Shown in His Creation

God's Word is powerful, and it still speaks today. Read this passage out loud:

> You made all the delicate, inner parts of my body
>   and knit me together in my mother's womb....
> You saw me before I was born.
>   Every day of my life was recorded in your book.
> Every moment was laid out
>   before a single day had passed. (Psalm 139:13, 16 NLT)

Take a breath and think about what this means for you. God's Word speaks into your story. It tells you of his loving and relentless pursuit of his people, of his loving and relentless pursuit of you. Think about your life, from your earliest memories until today. God knew every action, thought, and word before you were even born. God knew about your failures and mistakes, but amazingly, he still made you. There are things in your past of which you are ashamed. God knows those things. Nevertheless, he still knit you together. Why did he do so? God made you because he loves you and wants you to enjoy communion with him.

What Is Communion with God?

If you are struggling to understand your purpose in life, stop and consider why God made you. You are no accident. You were born so that you might enjoy God and have communion with him. Communion with God simply means how you experience your relationship with God. Communion with God involves three aspects: knowing, experiencing, and imaging. You can use the acronym KEI, pronounced like the word *key*, as a way of remembering these aspects.

Know. God wants you to have a personal relationship with him, where you know him and you are known by him. In the Hebrew language of the Old Testament, the verb *to know* didn't merely mean comprehending information about someone, but rather knowing them intimately.

Eternal life begins with knowing God personally and intimately. In John 17:3, Jesus prays to the Father with these words: "Now this is eternal life: that they know you, the only true God, and Jesus Christ, whom you have sent." God wants you to know him. He wants you to know his wisdom, kindness, and mercy, his presence, promises, and power. Later in that prayer, Jesus prays specifically that we might know God's love and glory as he has revealed himself in his word and by his Spirit.

Each of us desires to be known, to be heard, to be seen, and to know that we are loved. Not only did God personally and uniquely create you, but he knows you, hears you, and sees you. God loves you. Because God made you for an intimate relationship with him, he also created you to know him in return, and in a sense to hear him and see him also. He wants you to love him as well.

Experience. God designed you with a body and soul to experience him in deeply personal ways. God made you so that you can experience his beauty and love through what you see, smell, hear, taste, and touch. Moreover, God connected your soul and body seamlessly so that what impacts one part of you impacts all of you. When you're stressed, for instance about speaking in public, your mind floods with fears and worries. Your shoulders may lock with tension, and your stomach might feel uneasy. The stress that impacts your soul also impacts your body. But when you're enjoying time with someone you love such as a dear friend or spouse, you feel content and at ease. You may have more energy than normal or feel free to be silly. The love and joy you feel in your soul impact your body as well.

God designed your soul so that you can fully experience life and relationships. But more importantly, he made you to experience him with your thoughts, emotions, and desires. He designed you to understand his words, reason like him, and imagine his glory and beauty. He made you to feel joy and love in his presence, and he wants sorrow and anger to drive you to him for comfort and guidance. God also stirs your affections so that you will be compelled to live for him.

Imagine an unhurried walk outside. You feel the breeze brush past your skin as you hear the trees and bushes rustling with the wind. You smell a trace of wood smoke in the crisp air. Your eyes are drawn to the vibrant, multi-layered colors of the sunset which sends a tingle down your spine. When you drink this moment in with all of your senses, with all of your body, you're not merely experiencing the sensations of evening drawing near, but you are experiencing the goodness and beauty of your Creator. Your imagination, affections, and bodily sensations may stir in similar ways as you sit and reflect on a verse or truth in God's Word or when you sing the words of a favorite worship song.

Image. God wants you to reflect him by relating and responding according to his Word. In Genesis 1:26–27, we read, "Then God said, 'Let us make mankind in our image, in our likeness.' . . . So God created mankind in his own image, in the image of God he created them, male and female he created them." Being made in God's image is not a matter of physical appearance nor does it mean that humans are identical to God. Rather, being in God's image is about relating and responding to him in love-driven obedience.

We can struggle with knowing what to think, feel, and desire as we encounter different experiences in life. In our confusion, we can struggle to know what to do. We also have this innate longing to have someone we can look up to and learn from, who can guide us as we journey through life. Being made in the image of God means God serves as our counselor, our teacher, our guide, and our example. Jesus is the only person who can say, "Do as I say *and* do what I do." God created us to reflect him in how we live and love.

Knowing God enables us to live *with* him. Experiencing God compels us to live *for* him. Imaging God results as we live *like* him. Such a life not only gives us purpose for living but also gives direction for how we should live.

When we know and experience God's love, we are changed so that we can live reflecting God's image. That's how God designed us. Our bodies and souls are designed to respond to love in general and to God's love in particular. Like a flower responds to warm rays of sunlight, our hearts bloom in response to the deep, penetrating warmth of God's love. The apostle Paul describes it this way: "For Christ's love compels us, because we are convinced that one died for all, and therefore all died. And he died for all, that those who live should no longer live for themselves but for him who died for them and was raised again" (2 Corinthians 5:14–15).

To *compel* means to strongly urge or motivate. When you feel compelled, you just can't help yourself. Christ's love, demonstrated to us in his death and resurrection, *compels us* so that we just can't help but live for Jesus. God's faithful love for us in every moment of every day drives us to love and obey him.

RESPONSE ACTIVITIES (20 minutes)

Here is a selection of response questions and activities designed to stir your heart and soul and get you thinking deeply about the truths presented in this lesson. Write out your answers and reflections ahead of the group meeting, then be prepared to discuss your reflections together. **Consider your themes as you work through these questions.**

1. Proverbs 3:5–6 says, "Trust in the LORD with all your heart and lean not on your own understanding; in all your ways submit to him, and he will make your paths straight." Write down any truths from this lesson that convict and encourage you to trust God and submit to his understanding and ways instead of relying on your own understanding.

2. The psalmist writes, "How sweet are your words to my taste, sweeter than honey to my mouth!" (Psalm 119:103). Describe a time you tasted the sweetness of God as you read his Word.

3. Storyboard: Reflect for a moment on how and why God created you, and on your responses above. Then turn to the back of the book and fill out your storyboard thoughts on this lesson (page 184).

READ AND ABIDE: PSALM 139
(15 minutes of personal reflection, followed by 20 minutes of group discussion)

1. **Understand your reality.** Open your heart to God before you open the Word of God. How have others minimized or denied parts of your life story, or how have you ignored parts of it? Begin by telling these things to God, who takes all of your story seriously.

2. **Look up and see God's reality.** Read **Psalm 139** slowly one or two times. What do you find most amazing about how God created you? Include some ways he created you to have intimacy with him. Note any verses that stand out to you. (For example: "Verse 2—God knows my every move and my thoughts.")

3. **Understand your heart struggles.** Verses 7–12 say God is with you everywhere you go. This includes where you go or tend to flee in your fear or confusion. How do you struggle to believe that God is still with you even in those moments—that the darkness is not dark to him (v. 12)?

4. **Abide and rest in God.** Which part of the psalm most comforts you, and why?

5. **Follow God's invitation.** How is God answering the closing prayer to lead you "in the way everlasting" (v. 24)? In what way would God have you follow him today?

LOOK AHEAD (5 minutes)

List 1–2 practical ways you will seek to live differently this week based on God's invitation. Share your ideas with the group.

PRAYER (5 minutes)

Close out your time responding to God through prayer, giving him thanks for his faithfulness and love that you have experienced during the lesson and small group time. Ask for his Spirit to empower you to put into practice what he is teaching you so you can live and love differently.

LESSON 5
CREATION:
JESUS IS OVER ALL CREATION

BIG IDEA

Jesus is in control of everything in all creation, including your story—your meaning, your purpose, and everything that happens to you.

LOOK BACK (15 minutes)

Discuss among your group how God has enabled you to live differently, based on his invitation from the previous lesson's Read and Abide time.

THE BACKSTORY ON JESUS AND CREATION (10 minutes—Read aloud in group)

You might think Christ entered into our reality when he was born as a babe on Christmas. It's true that the Son was named Jesus and took on human flesh in order to be born at that Bethlehem stable, but the Bible also tells us that the Son of God is eternal and existed before the creation. In fact, it tells us that every aspect of God's created reality was brought into existence through the Son. Paul says it this way:

> The Son is the image of the invisible God, the firstborn over all creation. For in him all things were created: things in heaven and on earth, visible and invisible, whether thrones or powers or rulers or authorities; all things have been created through him and for him. He is before all things, and in him all things hold together. And he is the head of the body, the church; he is the beginning and the firstborn from among the dead, so

that in everything he might have the supremacy. For God was pleased to have all his fullness dwell in him, and through him to reconcile to himself all things, whether things on earth or things in heaven, by making peace through his blood, shed on the cross. (Colossians 1:15–20)

Nothing in creation was made apart from Christ, the Word. The apostle John confirms what we've read from Paul: "In the beginning was the Word, and the Word was with God, and the Word was God. He was with God in the beginning. Through him all things were made; without him nothing was made that has been made" (John 1:1–3).

Take a moment to reflect on the profound reality that Jesus Christ created "all things in heaven and on earth, visible and invisible, whether thrones or powers or rulers or authorities." Everything seen and unseen in God's created reality is under the absolute control of the Son of God. Imagine: every star, every species of animal, plant, and fish, every compound in the periodic table, every hue of color and tone of sound, every heart, lung, and brain function were created through the power and ability of Jesus.[3] The beauty and majesty of creation found in the distant universe, in far off lands, and in the human body and soul were made possible through Jesus.

Jesus Is Your Reference Point

Jesus is Lord over God's created order both now and into eternity. He is over all creation and human history in the past, in the present, and in the future. That includes you and your story. Because all things were made in him, there's no aspect of your created being that Jesus doesn't know about or understand. No matter your particular themes and struggles, Christ has every part of your reality covered.

As we live "below the clouds," God often seems distant and so disconnected from our reality. When life takes unexpected turns, we can become anxious and confused. But God is never caught off guard and he is never anxious. The Enemy seeks to use every aspect of our story to deceive us and to distort how we relate and respond to God as we wonder if he even knows us or cares for us.

God knows the battles we face, so he reminds us of his supremacy in all things. John tells us, "In him was life, and that life was the light of all mankind" (John 1:4). Jesus is not only our life but our light. In other words, *Jesus is our reference point*. Jesus knows that we wrestle with darkness and confusion. We can only understand who we are and what we are made for by knowing and experiencing him. We can only make sense of our reality and our story in light of Jesus's life and story.

When his disciple Thomas asked him, "Lord, we don't know where you are going, so how can we know the way?" Jesus answered, "I am the way and the truth and the life" (John 14:5–6). And later that same evening, Jesus told the disciples, "You did not choose me, but I chose you and appointed you so that you might go and bear fruit. . . . This is my command: Love each other" (John 15:16–17). Only he gives meaning and direction to our lives.

Jesus Is Your Purpose

The Colossians passage says all things were made not only through Jesus but also *for* him. Christ is the goal of all creation. Everything exists for Jesus—for his pleasure, joy, and glory. All creation testifies to him:

> The heavens declre the glory of God;
>   the skies proclaim the work of his hands.
> Day after day they pour forth speech;
>   night after night they reveal knowledge.
> They have no speech, they use no words;
>   no sound is heard from them.
> Yet their voice goes out into all the earth,
>   their words to the ends of the world. (Psalm 19:1–4)

Boys and girls are fascinated by the constellations on a pitch-dark night. People stand in awe while gazing at snowcapped mountain ranges or at the dark blue expanse of the oceans. We're captivated by the quiet glow of a sunrise and the radiant colors of a sunset. God made our souls to be stirred and inspired by his creation.

As we live in this visible world, we must remember it was made with an invisible purpose. The creation was made for more than we can see. All things, including us, were made for Jesus. We were made to live for him—for his pleasure, purposes, and praise—and not for ourselves.

What does it look like to live for Jesus? Does it mean we have to live like robots, saying every word Jesus says and doing every deed Jesus did? No, God doesn't want us to be like mechanical robots who are pre-programmed, where the builder dictates everything we say and do. But because we were created in his image, God does want us to reflect his character in how we live and love.

Jesus summarizes what it means to live for him: "Love the Lord your God with all your heart and with all your soul and with all your strength and with all your mind; and Love your neighbor as yourself" (Luke 10:27). Loving God with our whole being means that we live according to his word by obeying his commands—"If you love me, keep my commands" (John 14:15)—and that we love others by helping them to do the same. Such a life pleases God, fulfills his purposes, and brings him praise.

Jesus Holds All Things Together

The earth rotates around the sun at roughly 66,000 miles per hour. What keeps it from spinning off its orbit? The human heart beats more than 2.5 billion times over an average lifespan. What keeps it going? We take these functional realities for granted. But the Colossians passage tells us that behind it all, Jesus holds all things together. Both the laws of gravity and physics, as well as the life force behind all of our biological processes, are sustained "by his powerful word" (Hebrews 1:3).

Jesus not only keeps the visible and invisible realities of the creation in check, but he also works in all things to fulfill his purposes. What does this reality mean for you? Sometimes it seems as if your whole world is falling apart—your car, bank account, relationships, and even health. You may not have the energy or desire to get out of bed, to keep working, or to stay in your marriage. There may be moments when you believe that life isn't worth living. But Jesus still upholds your existence. He can and will sustain you through whatever presses you down. Jesus holds you together even when your world seems to be falling apart.

Why Does Evil Exist If Jesus Is Over All Creation?

Only God can fully explain why evil still exists. We do know that in the garden, before sin, there was the tree of the knowledge of good and evil. We know the evil angel, Satan, clashed in the heavens with God before being cast down to the earth. We also know there will be no evil in the new heaven and earth: "No longer will there be any curse" (Revelation 22:3). We live in a reality where good and evil coexist in every aspect of creation, including in every person. But there are three truths we can cling to: (1) God is holy, without any evil, (2) God conquered evil on the cross so that, (3) we can live with our sinless God through our union with Jesus Christ in this evil world.[4]

In later lessons, we will continue to unpack the tension between God's sovereign control over the heavens and earth and how evil seems to reign—the tension between God's love and our painful reality. But remember, the devil doesn't want us to believe in the supremacy of Jesus over all things. Instead, he wants us to believe the lies that God is not good, is not powerful, and doesn't love us.

For All These Reasons, Jesus Is Your Hope

Since all things were made through and for Jesus, it's possible for everything to be restored through him as well. "With God all things are possible" (Matthew 19:26). You may think your life is hopeless. You may doubt God can make a difference in your circumstances or relationships. But Christ is your life. Jesus, your Creator, invites you to place your hope in him. Look at him instead of your circumstances. Listen to his wisdom instead of worldly insight, trusting in his understanding instead of your own. Live in obedience to his word instead of doing what is right in your own eyes.

RESPONSE ACTIVITIES (20 minutes)

Here is a selection of response questions and activities designed to stir your heart and soul and get you thinking deeply about the truths presented in this lesson. Write out your answers and reflections ahead of the group meeting, then be prepared to discuss your reflections together. **Consider your themes as you work through these questions.**

1. Sometimes we limit Christ to the manger or the cross. How did God stir your imagination and heart as you reflected on the reality that all things in heaven and earth were created in, through, and for him?

2. Often it can seem as if your world is falling apart. Take some time to meditate on the two verses below.

   He is before all things, and in him all things hold together. (Colossians 1:17)

   The Son is the radiance of God's glory and the exact representation of his being, sustaining all things by his powerful word. (Hebrews 1:3)

How do these truths, and the other truths in this lesson, comfort you and help you to be more confident in God in spite of your current reality and struggles?

3. Storyboard: What is most encouraging to you about Jesus being over all creation? Turn to the back of the book and fill out your storyboard thoughts on this lesson (page 184).

READ AND ABIDE: PSALM 146
(15 minutes of personal reflection, followed by 20 minutes of group discussion)

1. **Understand your reality.** Open your heart to God before you open the Word of God. What part of your life feels out of control at the moment? Begin by telling God about it.

2. **Look up and see God's reality.** Read **Psalm 146** slowly one or two times. How does this psalm declare that Jesus, not the troubles of life, is in control and is your true reference point? Note any verses that stand out to you. (For example: "Verse 4—Powerful people die, but Jesus lives forever.")

3. **Understand your heart struggles.** What is hardest for you to believe is under God's control? It might be:
   - Your relationships, finances, health, etc. (v. 7–8)
   - Those who may have abandoned you or hurt you (v. 9)
   - Something else

Why do you think it's hard for you to believe God controls this part of your life?

4. **Abide and rest in God.** Verse 2 summarizes the psalm's message: it's about praising God in *all* of your life. How might God turn your worries to praise as you remember that he controls all things? What would that change look like in you?

5. **Follow God's invitation.** When you think of Jesus being your purpose in life, how does this prompt you to want to live differently for him or for others?

LOOK AHEAD (5 minutes)

List 1–2 practical ways you will seek to live differently this week based on God's invitation. Share your ideas with the group.

PRAYER (5 minutes)

Close out your time responding to God through prayer, giving him thanks for his faithfulness and love that you have experienced during the lesson and small group time. Ask for his Spirit to empower you to put into practice what he is teaching you so you can live and love differently.

LESSON 6
THE FALL:
EVIL KEEPS US FROM LOVE

BIG IDEA

Your life includes struggles against sin and evil, especially the struggle to believe and trust that God is good, loving, and in control.

LOOK BACK (15 minutes)

Discuss among your group how God has enabled you to live differently, based on his invitation from the previous lesson's Read and Abide time.

THE BACKSTORY ON THE FALL AND OUR HEART STRUGGLES (10 minutes— Read aloud in group)

God made you to be swept up into his never-ending love. He made you to enjoy deep, satisfying, and life-giving communion with the Father, Son, and Holy Spirit. In lesson 4, we learned how God made you with a body and soul so that you can know and experience his love. We also learned that he made you in God's image so that you might reflect him as you love him and others.

But, as a result of the fall, things are not how God intended them to be. Instead of dwelling in and enjoying God's presence and love, the first man and woman chose death over life, evil over good. And as a result of their sin, their intimate relationship with God was broken. God summarized their sins this way: "My people have committed two sins: They have forsaken me, the spring of living water, and have dug their own cisterns, broken cisterns that cannot hold water" (Jeremiah 2:13).

In our sin, we forsake God, who is our very life, and we seek to live in ways that only lead to emptiness. As a result, the evil in and around us seeks to keep us from love.

Consequently, brokenness and sin are everywhere. Sin's presence is everywhere and is in everyone, except in Jesus. Sin's promises are convincing and alluring. Sin's power is overwhelming and ruthless.

Our Heart Struggles

Our hearts struggle daily with sin and brokenness:

- First, we all face the same **common struggles** that Adam and Eve first faced after the fall. These struggles are described in lesson 1. All of us struggle, to some degree, with fantasy, guilt, shame, fear, anger, and sorrow in response to the evil within and around us.
- Second, we experience **relational struggles** with others. We can experience a wide range of relational brokenness—conflict, loneliness, anxiety, family dysfunction, physical abuse, manipulation, or even the death of loved ones. As a result, we might respond with distrust, self-protection, defensiveness, suspicion, isolation, or avoidance. We will explore how the fall impacts our relationships in lesson 7.
- Finally, we all wrestle with **faith struggles** as we strive to experience our communion with God. We may question God's control and care. We might believe lies about God. We can struggle to experience God's love, peace, and joy. We can struggle with a lack of desire for God and his Word. Later in this lesson, we will focus on our struggle to trust God.

Each of these struggles is complicated by what's at the core of our sinful nature—our consistent bent toward **self-love** and **self-glory**. We're also bent toward being lovers of ourselves, money, and pleasure "rather than lovers of God" (2 Timothy 3:4). We are all predisposed to exchange God's glory for our own or for the lesser glories found in creation (see Romans 1:21–23). Because we are made in God's image, we don't passively experience life, but we actively relate and respond to those around us in every circumstance.

HEART STRUGGLES

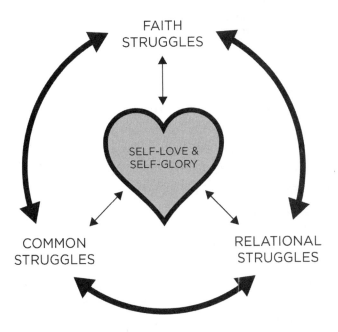

The diagram above shows the reciprocal nature of our struggles. Common struggles can lead to relational struggles, and relational struggles can stir up common struggles. Each of these can also lead to faith struggles, and our faith struggles can lead to common struggles or relational struggles. Each of these is connected to our core bent toward self-love and self-glory.

The Ongoing Reality of Spiritual Warfare

Further complicating the struggles of life is the fact that, in this broken world, an evil trinity—the **flesh**, the **world**, and the **devil**—wage war daily against God and his people. We call this *spiritual warfare*.

- Even as Christians, our sinful **flesh** battles against God's Spirit, prompting us to love ourselves more than loving God and others.
- The **world**, a culture that lives as if there is no God, feeds our insatiable desire to be the center of the universe.

- Our Enemy knows humanity's sinful condition and how susceptible we are to temptation. Nothing brings the **devil** greater joy than causing doubt and confusion in God's people.

Because this spiritual battle is invisible, more times than not we can forget about the presence and power of this warfare. Spiritual warfare targets our communion with God, undermining how we know and experience his love. To live victoriously, we must "be as shrewd as snakes and as innocent as doves" (Matthew 10:16). We need to be aware of and know the schemes of the Enemy, "in order that Satan might not outwit us" (2 Corinthians 2:11).

Satan has four primary schemes. He seeks to **deceive** us, to **distract** us, to **discourage** us, and to **divide** us, creating a break in our relationship with God and others.

- The Enemy **deceives** us with lies, tricking us into believing that God doesn't care about us or that his promises don't apply to us.
- The Enemy **distracts** us with worldly comforts and worry, tricking us into thinking more about our circumstances than about the God who dwells within us or the spiritual warfare that surrounds us.
- Satan **discourages** us, leading us to believe that nothing will change or that the bad outweighs the good in life.
- Often the Enemy's deception, distraction, and discouragement results in **division** between us and God or between us and one another.

Our Faith Struggles with God

The most crucial struggle to be aware of and to address is how we struggle to believe God. Without trust in God and his story, our view of reality will always be confused. So we need to understand how we all struggle in our relationship with God.

You may not even be aware that you are holding anything against God. Even if you are aware, you may be hesitant to acknowledge this struggle. And even if you are aware and acknowledge your struggles with God, you may not know how to address them, or have a desire to do so.

What do our faith struggles with God look like? These are the battles you might experience:

- **Battles with doubt.** You can doubt God's presence, promises and power. *God, where are you? God, do you care for me? Do you love me? I believe God's promises for others, but not for me. God, you can't change me... or my spouse. God, I doubt you can protect me or provide for me.*
- **Battles with despair.** When life changes for the worse and you can't see any light at the end of the tunnel, you can battle despair. Perhaps you notice that you have placed your hope in your circumstances or relationships changing. When they don't change you can battle hopelessness. *Why hasn't God changed me or my circumstances? Things will never change. Why won't God give me what I ask for?*
- **Battles with distance.** You can also think or feel that God is far from you. You might also turn your back on God and give up on him. This is a particular temptation when it seems he hasn't heard or answered your prayers. *How can I love a God who allowed _____? How can God love me after what I did? How can God love me after what was done to me? God doesn't hear/answer my prayers. God seems so far away.*

Anger with God

As doubts, despair, and distance harden your heart toward God, you might also become angry with him. Taking time to process what makes you angry is an essential part of spiritual warfare, knowing that while you are in darkness and pain, the enemy seeks to deceive you about God and divide you from him. Remember, anger is a strong feeling of displeasure or hostility in response to someone or something that opposes what you value.[5] This understanding of anger should cause you to pause and consider the reasons why you are angry with God. When we get angry with God, we can take one of two extreme stances.

First, we might accuse God of not being good. We can blame him for the evil in the world and the bad things that happen such as the death of a spouse or child, or a prolonged season of misfortune or misery, sickness, or loneliness.

Second, we might accuse God of not being loving. We accuse him of not caring, because we know he could have prevented the evil we experienced from happening or did not choose to give us what we wanted.

Faith Struggles Are Common, but Serious

We have to take our faith struggles seriously. Doubts, despair, and distance, if left unchecked, will take a toll on how we live and love. We will lack joy when doubts erode our trust in God. We will lack peace when despair drains any sense of hope. We will struggle to know and experience God's love when we think God is distant or when we hold God at a distance. As a result, some of us may become cynical, discontent, even numb, as we settle for just surviving. Or, we can seek to control every aspect of our lives, convinced that no one else can take care of us better than ourselves.

Let's consider the psalmist's confident reflection:

We wait in hope for the LORD;
   he is our help and our shield.
In him our hearts rejoice,
   for we trust in his holy name.
May your unfailing love be with us, LORD,
   even as we put our hope in you. (Psalm 33:20–22)

When we trust that God is our help and shield, we can rejoice. When we wait in hope for the Lord to work according to his promises, we can rejoice. When we are convinced of his unfailing love, we can rejoice.

How Do We Battle Against These Struggles?

We don't have a chance battling against these struggles on our own, because sin is more powerful than you and me. So, what can we do? We need to look up to see that our "help comes from the LORD" (Psalm 121:1) and to be reminded of the bigger reality in which we live. We need to look back to the creation story and remember the theme of God's love. It's impossible for God not to be loving. Because God's character is summed up by love, his activities are always loving and never wrong. We can also look ahead to the redemption story. God has revealed his love to us most profoundly at the cross: "While we were still sinners, Christ died for us" (Romans 5:8). Though we struggle with brokenness in our hearts, relationships, and faith, we can be confident that God will restore our brokenness through his story as we abide in Christ.

RESPONSE ACTIVITIES (20 minutes)

Here is a selection of response questions and activities designed to stir your heart and soul and get you thinking deeply about the truths presented in this lesson. Write out your answers and reflections ahead of the group meeting, then be prepared to discuss your reflections together. **Consider your themes as you work through these questions.**

1. Think about your daily battle to believe God. If you are aware of the spiritual warfare at play in your daily life, write down where the Enemy is at work to deceive, distract, discourage, or divide.

2. Think back to the themes and struggles of your story. Jot down any faith struggles you see in your journey. Do you battle doubt, despair, or distance from God? Are you angry with him?

3. Storyboard: Reflect on what you've learned about faith struggles, and then turn to the back of the book and fill out your storyboard thoughts on this lesson (page 184).

READ AND ABIDE: ISAIAH 55
(15 minutes of personal reflection, followed by 20 minutes of group discussion)

1. **Understand your reality.** Open your heart to God before you open the Word of God. What self-love and self-glory has consumed you recently? Begin by confessing this to your Father, who loves you even in your selfishness.

2. **Look up and see God's reality.** Read **Isaiah 55** slowly one or two times. What parts of God's invitation in this passage sound most compelling to you and make you want to come near to him? Why do they make you want to come near? Note any verses that stand out to you (for example: "Verse 1—I don't have to prove myself first. I can come empty-handed.").

3. **Understand your heart struggles.** How does your heart respond to God's invitation to draw near to him so that you can experience life, love, mercy, forgiveness, joy, and peace right now?

4. **Abide and rest in God.** How does this passage refute the lies the devil tells you about God and his word? Which truths in this passage settle your soul and give you rest?

5. **Follow God's invitation.** What are some sinful ways you need to forsake, or turn away from, as God invites you to draw near to him for life and love?

LOOK AHEAD (5 minutes)

List 1–2 practical ways you will seek to live differently this week based on God's invitation. Share your ideas with the group.

PRAYER (5 minutes)

Close out your time responding to God through prayer, giving him thanks for his faithfulness and love that you have experienced during the lesson and small group time. Ask for his Spirit to empower you to put into practice what he is teaching you so you can live and love differently.

LESSON 7
THE FALL:
TEMPTATION, SIN, AND BROKEN RELATIONSHIPS

BIG IDEA

Constant temptations are part of your life in this world, but temptations are also an opportunity for you to become more desperate for Jesus and dependent upon him.

LOOK BACK (15 minutes)

Discuss among your group how God has enabled you to live differently, based on his invitation from the previous lesson's Read and Abide time.

THE BACKSTORY ON OUR STRUGGLES WITH RELATIONSHIPS
(10 minutes—Read aloud in group)

God knows about the spiritual realities of the fall, and he has captured these realities in the pages of the Bible. Consider the story of David's temptation and his sin of sexual assault, as well as his attempt to cover it up through lying, scheming, and eventually the murder of an innocent man, all recorded in 2 Samuel 11 and 12.

One evening, David got up from bed and went on his rooftop, possibly to cool off during a warm night. He saw a beautiful woman bathing on an adjacent roof, and David was tempted. He sent one of his servants to find out about her. She was Bathsheba, the wife of one of his trusted soldiers, the daughter of one of his best fighters, and the granddaughter of his most trusted advisor.[6] Though he knew who she was, he sent messengers to get her so he could satisfy his sinful lusts. The temptation itself was not sin, but David sinned against God the moment he committed adultery in his heart. David continued to sin by taking Bathsheba and using her for his own pleasure.

Sometime later, Bathsheba sent word to David that she was pregnant. David furthered his sin by trying to cover it up with a series of lies and schemes. Eventually, David had Bathsheba's husband, Uriah, killed on the battlefield. After Bathsheba's time of mourning was over, David took her to be his wife, and she bore him a son. 2 Samuel 11 ends with this commentary: "But the thing David had done displeased the LORD." God later confronted David through the prophet Nathan, who declared, "Why did you despise the word of the LORD by doing what is evil in his eyes?" (2 Samuel 12:9).

The Temptation to Sin

Temptation is not necessarily sin. Even Jesus was tempted by the devil. Temptation is any invitation to turn away from God. External temptation leads to sin when a person gives into that temptation and turns away from God, despising his word by desiring and doing what is evil in God's eyes. Internal temptation reveals the desires of our sinful flesh and should be confessed as sin. Knowing that we will battle inward sinful desires and even external temptations until we get to heaven, we need to cultivate contrary affections informed by God's love and his Word.

When you give into temptation, you not only despise God's Word, but you also reject God (see 1 Thessalonians 4:8). Every sin—even when you sin against another person—is against God. God also describes sin as people doing "what was right in their own eyes" (Judges 21:25 ESV) rather than doing what is right in God's eyes. We sin when we lean on our own understanding (Proverbs 3:5) rather than trusting God and submitting to his ways.

David's Sorrow before His Confession

When we sin, we should confess those sins. David described the misery he felt before he confessed:

> When I refused to confess my sin
>   my body wasted away,
>   and I groaned all day long.
> Day and night your hand of discipline was heavy on me.
>   My strength evaporated like water in the summer heat. (Psalm
>   32:3–4 NLT)

Before David confessed, he suffered in part due to God's discipline. David also suffered from *worldly sorrow*—the remorse, self-condemnation, loathing, or despair that is mentioned in 2 Corinthians 7:10 and can come as a result of the shameful or painful consequences of sin.[7] David's misery may have flowed from his seared conscience—he knew he'd murdered a loyal soldier just to cover up his own lustful desires. Or his anguish could have resulted from guilt—David knew he deserved death according to God's law. Whatever the case, these feelings resulted from David's self-interest. Self-pity fuels worldly sorrow.

Godly sorrow, by contrast, expresses brokenness over sin, specifically sin against God. Once Nathan confronted David, God's Spirit convicted David and he confessed, "I have sinned against the LORD" (2 Samuel 12:13). While David had sinned against Bathsheba and her husband, and even against the servants and soldiers he used to cover up his sin, he knew his ultimate sin was against God. Through each of his sins against the others, David had despised God's commands and done evil in his sight. When David experienced godly sorrow, he was able to write the words of confession and repentance that we find in Psalm 51. That psalm is a picture of how true brokenness over sin leads to repentance. Repentance involves turning away from evil, and returning to God with trust and obedience.

David Experienced Sin's Consequences

Though David fasted before God and pleaded with him to heal his newborn child, his baby died seven days after birth. Even when we confess our sins to God and receive his forgiveness, this doesn't erase the consequences of sin (see Numbers 14:20–23).

It's the same with us. A man may be freed from the sinful habit of looking at pornography, but the images he has seen in the past can be etched in his memory and may reemerge when he least expects. Though a couple may reconcile after the husband commits adultery, his wife may struggle to trust him for some time. A woman who abused alcohol for decades may have to deal with ongoing health problems even though she has been sober for years. In each of these cases, the consequences are severe—but even so, repentance is worth it!

Use Temptations to Run to Jesus

There is no way to avoid the realities of the fall on this side of heaven. The Enemy won't cease his attacks. The world will continue tempting us to believe we can be satisfied apart from God. Our sinful flesh will continue to fight against God's Spirit within us. So, what can we do?

In the moment of temptation, flee to God. Paul tells Timothy, "Man of God, flee from all this, and pursue righteousness, godliness, faith, love, endurance and gentleness. Fight the good fight of the faith. Take hold of the eternal life to which you were called when you made your good confession in the presence of many witnesses" (1 Timothy 6:11–12).

When you are tempted to sin, don't give in to the lie that there is no way to escape the temptation. Such thinking will lead you to give in to further sin. When you are tempted to sin, don't lose heart by thinking that Christians should never struggle in this way or that you will never change.

Instead, use your temptations as merciful reminders that you desperately need Jesus. Use what the Enemy means for evil to instead turn your gaze toward Christ, who invites you to draw near to him for a peace that the world can't give and for a love that is better than life. See temptation as an opportunity to grow in humility before God and dependence upon him. Paul described it this way: "No temptation has overtaken you except what is common to mankind. And God is faithful; he will not let you be tempted beyond what you can bear. But when you are tempted, he will also provide a way out so that you can endure it" (1 Corinthians 10:13).

God doesn't promise to take away temptation, nor does he promise that we will not sin in our temptation. What God promises in this passage is that he will help you to endure in faith through any temptation without falling away from him or losing your salvation. Even if you must endure temptation for a lifetime, God only allows what will help you grow in humble dependence upon Christ. So, when you are tempted to sin, run to Jesus for refuge as you cry out to him through prayer. Run to Jesus through his Word so you can be reminded of his comforting presence and his life-giving promises. Instead of listening to the lies in your head or following the feelings in your heart, follow Christ through obedient faith so that you can abide in his love and experience his joy. He hasn't allowed more temptation to come your way than you can bear with his help. He stands ready to be your way of escape. And when you sin, whether by sinful desires or sinful actions, follow the example of David's confession and repentance in Psalm 51.

Broken Relationships

We experience the brokenness of this world most personally and painfully through our relationships. Just look at your own story, for instance. As you think about your different relationships in your family, or among your friends or coworkers or even those in your church, it doesn't take long before you can recall times of being disappointed or frustrated, lied to or rejected, judged or slandered. Conflict, avoidance, and division can be found in almost every relational realm in most people's life. Sadly, as you get to know the stories of those around you, you will also hear tragic relational trauma from neglect, abandonment, betrayal, abuse, human trafficking, even murder.

Relationships are broken from the way others have sinned against us, but also from the ways we have sinned against others. In other words, relationships are destined to fail whenever we consider ourselves and our interests as more important than others. Broken relationships hurt because they break our hearts.

The good news is that God not only addresses our struggle with broken relationships, but the gospel of Jesus Christ centers on him reconciling the ultimate broken relationship—the relationship between us and God. Not only can we be reconciled with God through the perfect and finished work of Jesus on the cross, but we can also be reconciled with one another by following Jesus, in the power of his Spirit, to forgive and love others in the same way he forgave and loved us. "Be kind and compassionate to one another, forgiving each other, just as in Christ God forgave you. Follow God's example, therefore, as dearly loved children and walk in the way of love, just as Christ loved us and gave himself up for us as a fragrant offering and sacrifice to God" (Ephesians 4:32–5:2).

RESPONSE ACTIVITIES (20 minutes)

Here is a selection of response questions and activities designed to stir your heart and soul and get you thinking deeply about the truths presented in this lesson. Write out your answers and reflections ahead of the group meeting, then be prepared to discuss your reflections together. **Consider your themes as you work through these questions.**

1. How might you be more aware of the dynamics of temptation and sin in your life as you consider the descriptions of temptation and sin in this lesson?

2. Sin damages and can even break relationships. Take a moment to consider the hurtful relationships in your life. Bring these relationships before God, asking him if there is any bitterness or unforgiveness in your heart. Take some time on your own to read through the additional reading, "Steps for Reconciling a Broken Relationship" that follows this lesson. Is there anyone with whom you need to reconcile? If so, consider sharing this with your group if you can do so without gossiping. Remember to focus on yourself and not the other person.

3. Storyboard: Think about your broken relationships and battles with temptation, and then fill out your storyboard thoughts on this lesson (page 184).

READ AND ABIDE: PSALM 51
(15 minutes of personal reflection, followed by 20 minutes of group discussion)

1. **Understand your reality.** Open your heart to God before you open the Word of God. What temptation, sin, or broken relationship is the Spirit of God convicting you about in this moment or season?

2. **Look up and see God's reality.** Read **Psalm 51** slowly one or two times. Look at how David confesses his sin and repents. Write down specific aspects of his confession and repentance. Note any verses that stand out to you. (For example: "Verse 4—He knew his sin was doing evil in God's sight.")

3. **Understand your heart struggles.** What makes confession and repentance difficult for you?

4. **Abide and rest in God.** Do you see your sin the same way David viewed his? How is God stirring your heart as you compare David's confession and repentance to how you typically confess and repent?

5. **Follow God's invitation.** How is God calling you to trust and obey him right now? Write out a prayer of confession.

LOOK AHEAD (5 minutes)

List 1–2 practical ways you will seek to live differently this week based on God's invitation. Share your ideas with the group.

PRAYER (5 minutes)

Close out your time responding to God through prayer, giving him thanks for his faithfulness and love that you have experienced during the lesson and small group time. Ask for his Spirit to empower you to put into practice what he is teaching you so you can live and love differently.

REFLECT AND PRAY: STEPS FOR RECONCILING A BROKEN RELATIONSHIP

The realities of the fall make relationships tough. It's hard to find and keep loving friends or stay connected to family members. God isn't blind to the hardships and heartache of our relationships. He knows we can experience deep hurt and even trauma in our relationships. Think about your own relationships. Is there a particular person—a roommate, family member, spouse, team member, neighbor, or coworker—with whom you have difficulty? Is there a particular relationship that feels distant, a person you avoid? Thankfully, God's Word does more than describe our relational difficulties, it also gives us concrete steps for reconciling broken relationships.

If a relationship comes to mind right away, it may be that you want to work through the hurt, address the awkwardness, speak truth in love, and pursue peace and unity. You may be ready to begin the reconciliation process outlined below.

Perhaps a person comes to mind, but they may have caused deep hurt through a given experience or over a season of time. Sometimes such painful encounters come from those we know and other times from strangers. Given your experience, you may not want to work through this guide, but remember that God knows your pain, your fears, your shame, even your bitterness. It's also possible that it would not be wise or safe at this time for you to try to reconcile with someone who has hurt you. In that case, ask a trusted friend, pastor, or counselor for their advice about the best way forward.

Because God loves you, he calls you to trust his words as you seek to follow him in ways that bring him glory and bring peace to your soul. "If your law had not been my delight, I would have perished in my affliction. I will never forget your precepts, for by them you have preserved my life" (Psalm 119:92–93).

God not only knows what you need. More than anyone else, he also knows how to shepherd and lead you through the brokenness of life and the resultant heartache. It's no coincidence that a major theme in God's story is Jesus as our Good Shepherd, who leads us on paths of righteousness, comforts us in the dark valleys of life, and keeps us in his love.

If there are no broken relationships that come to mind, take a moment to ask God to reveal anyone with whom you may need to reconcile. You might pray David's prayer from Psalm 139:23–24. "Search me, O God, and know my heart! Try me and know my thoughts. And see if there be any grievous way in me, and lead me in the way everlasting!"

Whatever your relational situation, the ultimate goal when we begin a reconciliation process is for everyone involved to grow in Christlikeness—that is, for all to learn to love and to forgive like him. Even if you are reconciling with someone who is not a Christian, your goal should be for them to see Christ's humility, love, and forgiveness through you.

Are you ready to work through the reconciliation steps? First read through the guide below. And as you do, pray and seek both God's wisdom and wisdom from others rather than rushing through this guide.

Step 1. Spend time with God. Make him your reference point.

Goal: Receive God's wisdom and look at your situation from God's perspective.

Too often, when we set out to address a broken relationship, we'll rely on our own understanding or others' opinions. But God wants to give us his wisdom. He offers it freely to everyone who seeks him.

Indeed, if you call out for insight
  and cry aloud for understanding—
and if you look for it as for silver
  and search for it as hidden treasure,
then you will understand the fear of the LORD
  and find the knowledge of God.

For the LORD gives wisdom;
   from his mouth come knowledge and understanding. (Proverbs
   2:3–6)

We are prone to look at our circumstances from the standpoint of what is best for us rather than what God says. A major theme in God's story is love. God created us to love and to be loved. In fact, Jesus summed up God's law in the two great commandments—love God and love your neighbor as yourself. One result of the fall is that we love ourselves instead of loving God and others. Jesus rescued us from ourselves so that we can love God and others as he did. In the new heaven and earth, we will be part of God's eternal family, and we will live and love in perfect oneness with Christ.

Step 2. Take an honest look at yourself. How well do you love God and others?

Goal: Grow in self-awareness and acknowledge how you can better love God and others.

Many times, others see us better than we see ourselves. That's especially true for those who spend the most time with us. And if we are aware of a weakness or failure, we can hesitate to acknowledge the issue because we're embarrassed, proud, afraid, or struggle with shame. Read **1 Corinthians 13:1–7** as a mirror to evaluate how you need to grow in love. Write down specific ways you need to grow in loving others in your journal.

Step 3. Consider these common relational mistakes.

Goal: Further grow in self-awareness by learning about some specific patterns that keep you from loving others well.

We develop patterns of relating to others based on our personal tendencies, family background, and life experiences. These habits are complicated by our sinful nature—our consistent bent toward self-glory and self-love. Consider the following relational mistakes that can hurt others even when that's not your intention. Note your tendencies. Then, ask a trusted friend to identify some tendencies you may have missed.

❏ **I lack awareness** of my own heart and the hearts of others.

❏ **I impose expectations** on others. When these aren't met, I get hurt and frustrated, and then lack love for others.

❏ **I make assumptions** instead of clarifying or seeking to understand others.

❏ **I accuse** others of being or doing wrong, based on what I think is right.

❏ **I get angry** when people don't agree with me or when they wrong or disappoint me.

❏ **I go on the attack**, hurting others with my words, attitude, and actions.

❏ **I avoid** dealing with pressing issues. This results in repeating the same arguments.

❏ **I don't rely on God**, but try to handle things in my own way.

❏ **I apologize** by merely saying "I'm sorry" rather than asking for forgiveness.

❏ **I avoid** others. I don't share what I'm dealing with.

❏ **I don't share** what's on my heart. I don't give thanks or celebrate when things go well.

So far, you have taken time to seek God's wisdom, make his love your reference, and discover how you need to grow in love by identifying some key relational mistakes. Now take time to pray so you can see how God is inviting you to confess. Confession is essential for reconciliation. God's call to reconciliation is not meant to be a burden. Rather, reconciliation is an opportunity for you to experience God's love in a deeper way. As you experience God's love and love others, his love will begin to restore the brokenness in your heart and soul.

Step 4. Express faith in God by confessing your sins.

Goal: Confess fully to God and others with a heart of humility and dependence.

Only Jesus loved others without relational sin. As you have worked through the first three steps, more than likely God has shown you some ways you have failed to love God and others in how you relate to them.

When you become aware of your sin, it's important to move toward God and others in confession.

First, confess to God. All sin is first and foremost against God. So, start with confessing to God how you have rejected his Word through your disobedience. Also confess how you have rejected God himself whenever you have trusted in your own understanding and tried to please yourself rather than please him.

Second, confess to others. Prayerfully consider the specific ways you have sinned as well as how that sin caused hurt and division. Then, (1) confess how you sinned against the other person, (2) share how you have hurt them, (3) ask them to share with you how you hurt them so that you can better understand the hurt you caused, (4) express sorrow for the hurt you caused and express what you would have done differently and how you will change.[8]

Step 5. Pursue peace by asking for and offering forgiveness.

Goal: Reconcile by loving and forgiving as Christ loved and forgave you (Ephesians 4:31—5:2).

You have done the hard work of looking up to God, looking in at your own heart, and owning what God has shown you to be your part in your relational brokenness. Be sure to ask the other person how you have hurt them.

When they share how you have hurt them, if they bring up additional issues or ways you have hurt them that you have not considered, you have two options. Either you can take the time to process in the moment, or ask if you can take some time to prayerfully ask God to search your heart and to help you to see what you need to see. After you have taken the necessary time, even if it means arranging to meet again, confess the additional ways you have sinned against them by working through the steps of confession.

After you confess to those you have failed to love, it's time to **ask for forgiveness**. You might say, "I am sorry for _____, I know I hurt you deeply, will you forgive me?" When you ask for forgiveness, you are in essence asking, "Will you love me despite how I have sinned against you?" Give the other person time to respond. Remember that you are responsible for your own confession and repentance, not their response.

You are not only responsible to ask for forgiveness but to pursue peace by **forgiving** the other person who sinned against you. Following Christ always means forgiving and loving like Christ. Jesus even calls us to love our enemies. If you are struggling to forgive, prayerfully read the parable of the unforgiving servant in Matthew 18:21–35. Remember that life and joy are found in trusting God's ways more than your own. Obey God and forgive rather than trusting your own thoughts, emotions, and desires. If the other person asks for forgiveness, forgive by saying, "Yes, I forgive you." When you forgive, you are in essence saying, "I commit to loving you despite your sins against me just as Jesus Christ loved and has forgiven me."

Forgiveness does not deny, excuse, accept, or allow the offense. It does not eliminate the consequences. It does not forget the memories. It does not imply reconciliation, since both parties need to do their part. It does not imply immediate restoration.

If each person confesses and asks for forgiveness, and then each person also forgives, then they have reconciled with one another.

If the other person does not repent and ask for forgiveness, the relationship is not reconciled. Here are further steps you can take:

- In obedience to Christ, you can forgive the unrepentant person (Matthew 6:14–15).
- Once you have repented, confessed, and asked for forgiveness, you can speak the truth in love, addressing the "speck" in the other person's eye.
- You can pray for God's Spirit to bring repentance to the other person so that you can reconcile.

If God enables the relationship to be reconciled, allow time before restoring the relationship.

In certain situations, you will need to ask God for wisdom before ever restoring the relationship. Situations such as abuse or reconciling with the "other man" or "other woman" in the aftermath of adultery require prayerful discernment. Even in such situations where restoration is not possible, God calls you to live without bitterness or hatred in your heart toward others. Rather, desire and pray for God's best for the other party—that they might know and experience God's love, which compels them to live for God instead of living for themselves.

Step 6. Restore the Relationship.

Goal: Experience again the love and oneness we enjoy in Christ (Ephesians 4:1–6).

A relationship can be reconciled after a time of mutual confession and forgiveness, but restoring a relationship requires time to rebuild trust and commitment. Rebuilding trust begins with placing your trust in God. Ongoing honesty and humility before God and one another are also necessary. Rebuilding commitment begins with an ongoing commitment to following Christ. One also must have a commitment to the unity and mission of the church.

Storyboard: What is God teaching you about reconciling relationships? Turn to the back of the book and record your thoughts on page 184.

LESSON 8
REDEMPTION:
JESUS RESTORES US WITH LOVE

BIG IDEA

Because of the suffering he endured, Jesus is both the Savior who died for your sin once for all and the Savior who can help you in every trial you face today.

LOOK BACK (15 minutes)

Discuss among your group how God has enabled you to live differently, based on his invitation from the previous lesson's Read and Abide time.

THE BACKSTORY ON JESUS'S LIFE ON EARTH (10 minutes—Read aloud in group.)

Think about a prevailing struggle you face each day. Perhaps, for instance, you battle persistent anxiety. If so, it's a part of your story. It may even be a theme in your story. But have you ever thought about where anxiety comes from in God's story? Let's think about it.

Were you created for anxiety? Of course not. Will you experience anxiety in the new heavens and new earth? No. Did Jesus come to increase your anxiety? Answering this question is tricky. It's true that if you see Jesus's life as the standard to which you must live, then that can cause you stress. Moreover, committing to follow Jesus in the midst of a hostile culture can cause you anxiety, too. Jesus himself said, "Do not suppose that I have come to bring peace to the earth. I have not come to bring peace, but a sword" (Matthew 10:34). But Jesus also said, "Do not let your hearts be troubled and do not be afraid" (John 14:27). And

Jesus makes clear that, in his redemptive work, he doesn't bring the kind of stress that can be associated with condemnation: "For God did not send the Son into the world to condemn the world, but to save the world through him" (John 3:17).

Ultimately, our anxieties—even the ones that Jesus's presence can increase—are rooted in the fall. That is good news! Why? Because the fall is not the end of God's story. You see, God knows every detail and dimension of our fallenness and brokenness, and he has a plan to address every one of our common struggles, relational struggles, and faith struggles.

When the Father sent the Son into our darkness, he came not only to reconcile us to himself but to restore us. Jesus enables us to love and to live fully human lives as he intended from the beginning. Jesus describes his own mission in this way: "The Spirit of the Lord is upon me, for he has anointed me to bring Good News to the poor. He has sent me to proclaim that captives will be released, that the blind will see, that the oppressed will be set free" (Luke 4:18 NLT).

God knew his people were helpless against the power of sin and blinded by the schemes of the Enemy. God knew his people could not save themselves. So, the Father sent his Son into the darkness of the fallen world to reconcile the division in our relationship with God and to restore the distortion in our souls, both caused by the sin in and around us.

Jesus Entered Our Darkness

Jesus willingly obeyed his Father even though he knew the great humiliation, trauma, and death he would suffer in order to rescue God's people. John describes it this way: "In the beginning was the Word, and the Word was with God, and the Word was God. He was with God in the beginning. Through him all things were made; without him nothing was made that has been made. In him was life, and that life was the light of all mankind. The light shines in the darkness, and the darkness has not overcome it. . . . The true light that gives light to everyone was coming into the world" (John 1:1–5, 9).

John refers to the creation story to help us see the extraordinary lengths God went to. God sent his Son into the world the Son himself had made. But "though the world was made through him, the world did not recognize him. He came to that which was his own, but his own did not receive him" (John 1:10–11). Why did people respond to Jesus in this way? John explains, "Light has come into the world, but people loved darkness instead of light because their deeds were evil" (John 3:19). The darkness of sin reoriented humanity's understanding and affections. Instead of knowing God and loving God with all of their heart, soul, mind, and strength, people have loved darkness and hated the light "for fear that their evil deeds will be exposed" (v. 20).

Jesus Is Fully Human

When the Son entered our world, he became fully human, though without sin. Jesus took a body and soul like ours. The author of Hebrews describes it this way:

> Since the children have flesh and blood, he too shared in their humanity so that by his death he might break the power of him who holds the power of death—that is, the devil—and free those who all their lives were held in slavery by their fear of death. . . . For this reason, he had to be made like them, fully human in every way, in order that he might become a merciful and faithful high priest in service to God, and that he might make atonement for the sins of the people. Because he himself suffered when he was tempted, he is able to help those who are being tempted. (Hebrews 2:14–15, 17–18).

Jesus humbled himself by sharing in our humanity. We marvel when celebrities, athletes, or presidents take the time to visit children in the hospital or serve lunch in a homeless shelter. But Jesus went much further. He took on our very nature to break Satan's power and become a merciful and faithful high priest.

Jesus Learned Obedience through Suffering

Jesus's time on earth was not like a presidential visit. He was not honored nor treated as a dignitary. Rather, his life on earth was filled with humiliation and suffering. He suffered through temptation in the wilderness. He suffered in the garden of Gethsemane. And he faced the most extraordinary test a person can experience on the cross. Jesus endured this life of suffering, yet sustained his communion with the Father and Spirit through desperate and dependent prayer. "He offered up prayers and petitions with fervent cries and tears" (Hebrews 5:7).

Jesus "learned obedience from what he suffered and, once made perfect, became the source of eternal salvation for all who obey him" (Hebrews 5:8–9). This does not mean that Jesus turned from disobedience to obedience, but that he lived a sinless life on earth. Through various seasons of trials, he demonstrated over and over his absolute trust and obedience to his Father. Through every temptation thrown at him by the devil, he lived with unwavering submission to God. And through each and every hardship, his obedience testified to his perfection so we might see him as the only source of eternal salvation.

Jesus Suffered Unlike Anyone Else on the Cross

Jesus suffered greatly even before the crucifixion. He was despised and rejected by the very people he created. As he came near the cross, they further afflicted him verbally and physically, so that "his appearance was so disfigured beyond that of any human being" (Isaiah 52:14). Then on the cross, he suffered his greatest trial.

Others have suffered physically in ways similar to Jesus through bodily torture; two thieves were crucified next to him. But Jesus experienced ultimate suffering for three reasons:

First, Jesus took upon himself the sins of the whole world. (1 John 2:2). Consider the burden you feel when you've done something wrong. The sense of guilt and disgust can be more than you can handle. Now, multiply what you experience personally by the number of people in the world throughout human history. Imagine what Jesus must have experienced. Paul says, "God made him who had no sin to be sin for us, so that in him we might become the righteousness of God" (2 Corinthians 5:21).

Second, Jesus absorbed God's wrath. Jesus absorbed the fury of God's wrath that was due for our transgressions. He endured the full measure of God's righteous anger against our sin until God's holiness and justice was fully satisfied. He did this so we might be restored. Isaiah prophesied these words about Jesus: "He was pierced for our transgressions, he was crushed for our iniquities; the punishment that brought us peace was on him, and by his wounds we are healed" (Isaiah 53:5).

Finally, Jesus was forsaken by the Father. Darkness covered the land, starting at noon, as Jesus bore the crushing weight of the world's sin and suffered the unbearable torment of God's wrath. At the end of three hours, he cried out in agony and anguish, "My God, my God, why have you forsaken me?" (Matthew 27:46). This cry was not a declaration of doubt about the Father's love, nor was it a cry of confusion about what he was experiencing. But for a moment never to be repeated, the Father turned his face away from his Son—not out of displeasure (because Jesus perfectly obeyed his Father's will) but because God's "eyes are too pure to look on evil" (Habakkuk 1:13). At that moment, Jesus did not consciously experience the deep, intimate fellowship he'd always known and enjoyed.

Let's not miss the beauty amid the darkness. Two realities were true at this moment: First, as Charles Spurgeon put it, "Jesus Christ was forsaken of God because we deserved to be forsaken of God."[9] Jesus willfully suffered temporary separation from God so that we would not suffer eternal separation and can cry out with confidence that nothing "will be able to separate us from the love of God that is in Christ Jesus our Lord" (Romans 8:39).

Second, before he took his final breath, Jesus also called out, "Father, into your hands I commit my spirit" (Luke 23:46). This cry revealed his unwavering trust in the guardian of his soul and his confidence that he would once again experience the sweet, intimate communion with God. As John Piper reflects, Jesus "had embedded in his soul both the horrors of the moment of abandonment, and he had embedded in his soul 'for the joy that was set before him.'"[10]

All that Jesus suffered on the cross should convince us that he is the perfect high priest, the only one who can fully identify with all of the injustice, heartache, affliction, sorrow, and trauma we might ever experience in this evil world. Jesus personally understands and relates to our pain unlike anyone else. Not only does Jesus understand our burdens and brokenness, but he is the only one able to bear our burdens and bind up our brokenness. And the Father's love and faithfulness to Jesus the Son, even when Jesus cried out, "My God, my God, why have you forsaken me?" should inspire hope in us that God loves us and remains faithful to us even during our darkest pain.

The Trials of Life

Life in a fallen world is filled with trials. Trials can include both temptations and testing. It is important to know the difference between the two. Temptations invite you to turn away from God to desire or do evil. Testing, however, is an invitation to trust and obey God. God tests us, but James 1:13 says he never tempts us. He always invites us to trust and obey him, never luring us towards evil. Nevertheless, a test and temptation can come together. What Satan intends for evil, God intends for good. Just ask Joseph or Job.

Trials can be situational—lasting only for a moment—or last a season. They can even last for a lifetime. Throughout Israel's history, we see God testing his people to reveal whether or not they love him with all their heart and soul (Deuteronomy 13:3). God's purpose in testing his people is to grow them in humility before him and dependence on him.

Remember this as you consider the trials in your life. *We learn obedience through suffering, just like Jesus did.* Trials are opportunities for you to learn to trust and obey God.

Paul describes it this way: "We do not want you to be uninformed, brothers and sisters, about the troubles we experienced in the province of Asia. We were under great pressure, far beyond our ability to endure, so that we despaired of life itself. Indeed, we felt we had received the sentence of death. But this happened that we might not rely on ourselves but on God, who raises the dead" (2 Corinthians 1:8–9).

God uses all our struggles and suffering, trials and troubles, to teach us to rely on him for everything. As we depend on him more and more, we experience the heights and depths of his love (Ephesians 3:17–19). We live in his unsurpassed peace even when our circumstances don't change (Philippians 4:7). And we become convinced that his nearness is our goodness (Psalm 73:28). In God's wisdom, when we are compelled by the love of Christ, we no longer rely on ourselves but live for him who died for us and was raised from the dead (2 Corinthians 5:14–15).

Jesus restores us with love so that we are free to love. Even as we live in a broken world, evil no longer has the power to keep us from love as we live in union with love himself and the Spirit of love dwells in us. Only Jesus Christ can truly change how we live and love.

RESPONSE ACTIVITIES (20 minutes)

Here is a selection of response questions and activities designed to stir your heart and soul and get you thinking deeply about the truths presented in this lesson. Write out your answers and reflections ahead of the group meeting, then be prepared to discuss your reflections together. **Consider your themes as you work through these questions.**

1. The Father sent his Son, the creator of the universe, to live among us. Jesus, the light of the world, came into our darkness, but we rejected him. Jesus took our flesh and blood, becoming fully human in body and soul. But we neither recognized nor received him. Where do you see God's glory and love through this portion of God's story?

2. How does the reality of Jesus entering the fall help you know and experience God's love and deepen your trust in Christ?

3. Reflect on the trials, both large and small, that you have faced recently. In the midst of those trials, where do you tend to look for help? Jot down answers to the following questions and be prepared to share them with your group.

   • Who and what do you listen to when seeking help—friends, blogs, podcasts, books, your own heart, your relentless thoughts, overwhelming emotions, dominating desires, etc.?

   • How do you tend to live in response to your trials—in fear, overwhelmed, scheming to fix the problem, staying awake at night because your mind won't turn off, relying upon yourself to survive, etc.?

4. Storyboard: Turn to the back of the book and fill out your storyboard thoughts on this lesson (page 185), and the redemption Jesus accomplished for you.

READ AND ABIDE: ISAIAH 52:13–53:12
(15 minutes of personal reflection, followed by 20 minutes of group discussion)

1. **Understand your reality.** Open your heart to God before you open the Word of God. What trials or sufferings are weighing on you right now? Tell them to God. Jesus understands your trials and sufferings.

2. **Look up and see God's reality.** Carefully read **Isaiah 52:13–53:12,** which tells of Jesus's suffering. Note two things: (1) What words might you use to describe Jesus's suffering? (2) How does his suffering benefit you? Note any verses that stand out to you. (For example: 53:9—His suffering was undeserved. 53:10—It was an offering for my sin.)

3. **Understand your heart struggles.** How does your heart respond to the truths and benefits of Jesus's suffering as you noted above? If your heart is hardened, indifferent, or hopeless, ask God to help you to see the depths of your sins and the heights of his love.

4. Abide and rest in God. When you experience sufferings and trials, how might they lead you to rely on Jesus more or take greater comfort in what he has done for you?

5. Follow God's invitation. Think of a suffering or trial that could become an opportunity for you to obey God or love him better? What is it, and how can you love and obey?

LOOK AHEAD (5 minutes)

List 1–2 practical ways you will seek to live differently this week based on God's invitation. Share your ideas with the group.

PRAYER (5 minutes)

Close out your time responding to God through prayer, giving him thanks for his faithfulness and love that you have experienced during the lesson and small group time. Ask for his Spirit to empower you to put into practice what he is teaching you so you can live and love differently.

LESSON 9

REDEMPTION:

WE LIVE IN GOD'S PRESENCE

BIG IDEA

God's redeeming work for you did not end with the cross, but continues today as you abide in him and he abides in you.

LOOK BACK (15 minutes)

Discuss among your group how God has enabled you to live differently, based on his invitation from the previous lesson's Read and Abide time.

THE BACKSTORY ON LIVING IN GOD'S PRESENCE (10 minutes—Read aloud in group.)

Even as Christians, we sometimes lack confidence in our salvation. If we have a chronic sin struggle, for instance, we can question whether or not the Holy Spirit is really working in us. We may also question God when we've pleaded with him to change us or our circumstances but nothing changes. When we doubt like this, we can live defeated lives, convinced we're alone and helpless.

As our Creator and Redeemer, is this how God sees our lives? No! *God is confident in his salvation plan.* Read these words from Jeremiah:

This is what the LORD says:
"'Your wound is incurable,
your injury beyond healing.
There is no one to plead your cause,

no remedy for your sore,
   no healing for you. . . .
Why do you cry out over your wound,
   your pain that has no cure?
Because of your great guilt and many sins
   I have done these things to you. . . .
But I will restore you to health
   and heal your wounds,"
     declares the Lord. (Jeremiah 30:12–13, 15, 17)

God speaks bluntly about his people's condition; he doesn't sugarcoat it. From a human perspective, their wound is incurable. But what is impossible with man is possible with God. Though there is no human remedy, God confidently declares that he is able to restore his people to health and heal their wounds.

Your incurable wounds—created by your own sin, the sins committed against you, and the brokenness caused by the fall—are not beyond God's healing power.

What God says he will do, he does. Guaranteed. How can God promise that nothing "will be able to separate us from the love of God" (Romans 8:39)? How can God take your story and bring "a crown of beauty instead of ashes" (Isaiah 61:3)? These and other questions have a simple answer. God's presence, promises, and power are not dependent on who you are, what you do, what you haven't done, or what was done to you. God freely and intentionally carries out his redemptive work in you based on who he is, what Christ has done, and what God's Spirit will do.

If God is confident in his salvation, you can be confident as well. Let's look at four reasons God's plan of redemption can't be ruined by anyone, not even you.

1. **God redeemed you by the perfect work of his Son.** After the first man and woman rebelled against God, sin took root in humanity's DNA. Your flesh is defiant, defiled, and disordered. You can't know God nor live for him apart from his powerful

grace. God knew you were helpless and hopeless, so he sent his Son to die and rise and redeem you fully. God's powerful work of redemption brought you from death to life. Now, God works to transform you so that you can be compelled and ruled by God's love rather than self-love; you can seek and live for God's glory rather than self-glory.

2. **God united you to Christ.** God has forgiven your sins and declared you not guilty through the cross of Jesus Christ. That redemption reality brings you into union with Christ—the intimate and inseparable relationship you have with the Son. The very moment God saved you, he transferred you out of the kingdom of darkness and "into the kingdom of the Son he loves" (Colossians 1:13). Jesus gave us an illustration of our union with him as he described himself as the Vine—our source of life—and us as the branches. By faith in Christ, you have been grafted into him. When God saved you, he made you a new creation (2 Corinthians 5:17). You can now claim his story as your own. "You died, and your life is now hidden with Christ in God. When Christ, who is your life, appears, then you also will appear with him in glory" (Colossians 3:3–4). Your oneness with your Redeemer never changes. You didn't do anything to earn this union nor can you do anything to mess it up.

3. **God gave you his Spirit.** The prophet Ezekiel gave us this promise about the new-covenant work of the Holy Spirit: "I will sprinkle clean water on you, and you will be clean; I will cleanse you from all your impurities and from all your idols. I will give you a new heart and put a new spirit in you; I will remove from you your heart of stone and give you a heart of flesh. And I will put my Spirit in you and move you to follow my decrees and be careful to keep my laws. Then you will live in the land I gave your ancestors; you will be my people, and I will be your God." (Ezekiel 36:25–28). When you were redeemed and united with Christ, God poured out his love into your heart "through the Holy Spirit, who has been given to us" (Romans 5:5). With the Holy Spirit

living within you, you have a new heart, empowering you to love God with your entire being—your thoughts, emotions, desires, and actions. God's Spirit now moves through your affections. As you receive God's love, you are compelled to live for him rather than for yourself, trusting and obeying him because you delight in him, not merely because it is your duty.

4. **The Son and Spirit pray for you.** God the Son and God the Holy Spirit offer prayers for you without interruption. They serve as your advocates before the Father right now. In your times of weakness when you don't know what to pray or how to pray, you can remember that God's Holy Spirit prays for you "with groanings too deep for words" (Romans 8:26 ESV). And when you sin or fear condemnation, know that you "have an advocate with the Father—Jesus Christ the Righteous One" (1 John 2:1). If you are gripped by fear and anxiety, trapped in dark sorrow, covered with a blanket of shame or guilt, lingering in fantasy more than reality, simmering in low-grade anger, or even boiling over in explosive rage, take comfort. "Christ Jesus who died— more than that, who was raised to life—is at the right hand of God and is also interceding for us" (Romans 8:34).

These realities should make us confident in God's redemption—as confident as God himself is in his salvation plan (see Jeremiah 32:40–41). But the realities of our redemption don't always feel real or true to us day by day. Too often we can dismiss or minimize God's reality when our doubts overshadow our faith, when hopelessness looms in our chronic suffering, or when God's love seems distant in our battle with sin. We should not see life as either good or bad. We tend to conclude that if life is hard, then God is not good.

But in God's story, we live in Christ as we live in a fallen world. We can be in union with Christ but still experience the daily struggles of evil in and around us. Here's the point that we need to remember: God's realities and the fall's realities can be true at the same time.

In the midst of these struggles, how can we grow in a greater awareness of God's presence? How can we live with more assurance and confidence in God and his story of restoration?

Living in God's Presence

Even though your union with Christ is steadfast and never changes, your communion with God—how you experience your relationship with God—ebbs and flows like the ocean tides. At times, you may sense Jesus is close to you and feel deep affection for him. At other times, you feel numb, dried out, and confused about your relationship with God.

Jesus knows that we struggle to feel his presence, so he invites us to draw near to him—to abide with him. God's time-tested way of deepening how you experience your relationship with him is through receiving, praying, and living out God's word by God's Spirit, both personally and communally with God's people.

God invites you to hunger and thirst for his righteousness, and when you do, he promises to satisfy you (Matthew 5:6). He invites you to draw near to him and find rest (Matthew 11:28–30). This invitation for us to come into Christ's presence is radical. In the Old Testament, God told his people not to step foot on Mount Sinai lest they be consumed by fire and die. Even at the tabernacle, where God came down to meet with his people, only the high priest could enter the Most Holy Place and he could only enter it once each year. But now, Jesus gives us an open invitation into his presence. He tells us to boldly and confidently approach his throne "so that we might find mercy and grace to help us in our time of need" (Hebrews 4:16).

You Can Live Differently in God's Story

The Enemy wants you to think that your past defines you—that you, or your life, will never change. If you keep your eyes only on your story and the pain and suffering you have experienced, or if you keep focused on your chronic struggles that have defeated you time and time again, then you will find yourself cynical or even hopeless. Your life will either stay the same or just get worse.

You may be convinced that God doesn't love you or care about you because of what you have gone through.

If your past and pain remain bigger and more present than God, not only will you sink into despair, but your heart will harden toward God either through outright rejection or through subtle, yet dangerous, apathy or numbness.

Don't be convinced by the lies. Don't be distracted by the ways of the world. Look up and remember that you are united with Christ, who not only created heaven and earth but created you with love and for love. Don't lose heart and grow weary. The Spirit of God dwells in you, reminding you of God's truths and promises and empowering you in your weakness. The Son and the Spirit are pleading to the Father on your behalf so that you will keep your eyes on Christ for hope and peace.

Jesus invites you to come to him so he can give you rest. Commit to trust him rather than your own understanding by following Christ as he shepherds you. Live differently by faith through the power of his Spirit.

Take some time now to explore the practical benefits of living in God's presence by working through the response activities.

RESPONSE ACTIVITIES (20 minutes)

Here is a selection of response questions and activities designed to stir your heart and soul and get you thinking deeply about the truths presented in this lesson. Write out your answers and reflections ahead of the group meeting, then be prepared to discuss your reflections together. **Consider your themes as you work through these questions.**

1. One benefit of God's presence is that it gives us **perspective.** When we open God's Word, he clarifies our confusion (Psalm 73:16–17). He enables us to see and trust him.

   • You may feel alone, but the Word reminds you that *Jesus is with you.* "Surely I am with you always, to the very end of the age" (Matthew 28:20).

   • God may seem like a mirage, but the Word reminds you that *God is real.* "Without faith it is impossible to please God, because anyone who comes to him must believe that he exists and that he rewards those who earnestly seek him" (Hebrews 11:6).

- You may think God is nowhere to be found, but *he is pursuing you with his love*. "Surely your goodness and love will follow me all the days of my life" (Psalm 23:6).

- You may wonder if God cares, but *he carries you, holding you close to his heart*. "He gathers the lambs in his arms and carries them close to his heart; he gently leads those that have young" (Isaiah 40:11).

- God may seem far away, but *Jesus invites you*, "Come to me, all you who are weary and burdened, and I will give you rest" (Matthew 11:28).

- He may not feel near, but *you're in Christ and he's in you*. Jesus said, "you will realize that I am in my Father, and you are in me, and I am in you" (John 14:20).

- Reality may appear too dark for you to see his beauty, but *the heavens still declare* it. "The skies proclaim the work of his hands" (Psalm 19:1).

Do you tend to doubt God's presence? Write down your specific doubts. Then pray and ask God to deepen your faith so that you can trust him rather than your feelings.

2. Another benefit of God's presence is that it gives **life** and **hope.** Meditate on these realities.

- God's presence is *your good*. "But as for me, God's presence is my good" (Psalm 73:28 CSB).

- Jesus is the vine and, through union with him, you are a branch. *His life flows through you.* "If you remain in me and I in you, you will bear much fruit" (John 15:5).
- Your shepherd is with you, *renewing and restoring your soul.* "He makes me lie down in green pastures, he leads me beside quiet waters, he refreshes my soul" (Psalm 23:2–3).
- The God of all comfort is with you, *comforting you in all of your troubles.* "Praise be to the God and father of our Lord Jesus Christ, the father of compassion and the God of all comfort" (2 Corinthians 1:3).
- In God's presence, there are *eternal pleasures and fullness of joy.* "You will fill me with joy in your presence, with eternal pleasures at your right hand" (Psalm 16:11).

Are you are drowning in despair? Which image from the above realities gives you most hope and comfort?

Take this truth with you this week. Remember that Jesus, your living hope (1 Peter 1:3), is with you every moment of every day.

3. God's presence also leads to **obedience** and **joy.** "As the Father has loved me, so have I loved you. Now abide in my love. If you keep my commandments, you will abide in my love, just as I have kept my Father's commandments and abide in his love. These things I have spoken to you, that my joy may be in you, and that your joy may be full" (John 15:9–11 ESV). Just as the Father loved Jesus, God also loved us before we loved him. But in this passage, Jesus tells us that God's love for us

stirs our love for him so that we respond with love-driven obedience. Obedience to his commands is necessary for us to experience his joy.

Does God feel distant to you? Are you simply walking through a dry spell in your communion with God, or could it be that you have turned your back on God? Are there sins that you need to confess? If so, take some time to list them. Write out a prayer of confession, and trust that God offers forgiveness for every sin.

4. Since obedience is the pathway to joy, is there a particular way God is calling you to trust or obey him right now?

5. Storyboard: Reflect on what God has shown you in this lesson, and record it on the lesson 9 section of your storyboard in the back of the book (page 185).

READ AND ABIDE: PSALM 84

15 minutes of personal reflection, followed by 20 minutes of group discussion)

1. **Understand your reality.** Open your heart to God before you open the Word of God. How does your communion with God feel? Is it close or distant? Joyful or humdrum? Tell God about it.

2. **Look up and see God's reality.** Carefully read **Psalm 84**, which expresses a longing for God's temple that turns out, in the final verses, to be a deep desire for God himself. What kind of communion with God does this psalm offer and show to be possible? Note any verses that stand out to you. (For example: "Verse 1—Being in God's presence is lovely and beautiful.")

3. **Understand your heart struggles.** What do you find hard to believe that keeps you from feeling close to God? It may be:
   - That God is your good Father who loves, cares, gives, listens, disciplines, etc.
   - What Christ has done for you
   - What the Spirit will do in you

4. **Abide and rest in God.** List the ways Psalm 84 reminds you of how God created you to live with him and how he intends to work in you.

5. **Follow God's invitation.** What might you do to come closer to God right now? This week? As an ongoing practice?

LOOK AHEAD (5 minutes)

List 1–2 practical ways you will seek to live differently this week based on God's invitation. Share your ideas with the group.

PRAYER (5 minutes)

Close out your time responding to God through prayer, giving him thanks for his faithfulness and love that you have experienced during the lesson and small group time. Ask for his Spirit to empower you to put into practice what he is teaching you so you can live and love differently.

LESSON 10
REDEMPTION:
WE LIVE IN GOD'S PROMISES

BIG IDEA

When life feels unsure, God's promises are sure: he will always be with you and always love you perfectly.

LOOK BACK (15 minutes)

Discuss among your group how God has enabled you to live differently, based on his invitation from the previous lesson's Read and Abide time.

THE BACKSTORY ON LIVING IN GOD'S PROMISES (10 minutes—Read aloud in group.)

Have you ever thought about the word *amen* that we say at the close of our prayers? Do you know the significance of that word, or do you simply say it because that's what you've been taught? "Amen" comes from a Hebrew word that means "this is true," "I agree," or simply "yes!"

Do you ever find yourself saying "amen" when you hear God's Word preached, taught, or sung? If you've been around church culture long enough, it may begin to flow from your mouth anytime God's truth resonates deep within your soul. Every time you say "amen," you are expressing confidence that God is faithful to what he has said. You're saying, "I believe what God says is true." It stirs your heart and then it bubbles up and out.

In 2 Corinthians 1:20–22, the apostle Paul describes Jesus as our Yes and Amen: "For no matter how many promises God has made, they are 'Yes' in Christ. And so through him the 'Amen' is spoken by us to the glory of God. Now it is God who makes both us and you stand firm in Christ. He anointed us, set his seal of ownership on us, and put his Spirit in our hearts as a deposit, guaranteeing what is to come."

God knows every detail and dimension of our lives, from the frenzy of our daily activities to the anguish swirling deep in our hearts. There is not a single moment or a solitary place where we can escape from his Spirit. God is not only with us in all our struggles, but he invites us to draw near to him for refuge. When the Father sent the Son into the realities of the fall, he came not only to reconcile us to himself but also to restore us from all of the ways evil has distorted our lives, damaged our souls, and devastated our relationships.

Paul reminds us that God's promise of redemption and restoration is fulfilled through the life, death, and resurrection of Jesus Christ. We may struggle to trust that God's promises are true. We may lack confidence or assurance that God's Word addresses our specific needs or the reality of our story, but Jesus remains faithful to his promises even when we don't feel it.

At the end of God's story, Jesus will ride in on a white horse as the great hero and promise keeper. Revelation 19:11 tells us his name, Faithful and True, will be written on his side. Until that day, God has given us his Holy Spirit as a down payment and guarantee that his promises will be kept both now and forever. Whenever we say "amen," we give God glory for being the Faithful One who both keeps his commitment to begin his restoring work in us now and will complete it upon his return.

God's Promises Give Us Confidence in the Battle

The Enemy does everything he can to destroy your confidence in God's love and his Word. Satan seeks to undermine your trust in God and his promises. How many times have you heard yourself or someone else say, "I don't know what is true or what is real anymore." "How can I trust God after what happened to me?" "Why should I care about God when he doesn't seem to care about me?" "He doesn't seem to hear or answer my prayers." "I don't know what to pray anymore—or if prayer even makes a difference." When we don't look to God for help or when we fail to listen to God's Word, we are like ships in a storm, tossed back and forth by the wind and waves of doubt.

But when we are overwhelmed with doubt, confusion, and a growing sense that we can't trust God, we should remember the following things that God will never do. He counters every one of Satan's attacks.

- God will never **deceive** you, because God doesn't lie (Numbers 23:19).
- God will never **distract** you from reality. He wants you to face reality by seeking him (1 Chronicles 16:11; Psalm 27:8).
- God will never **discourage** you. He promises joy for those who trust and obey him (John 15:9–11).
- God will never **divide** or separate you from himself. He's brought you into an unbreakable covenant relationship with himself through your union with Christ (Galatians 2:20).

In the midst of the battle, look to Jesus and remember all that God has promised you. Unlike the empty promises of sin, God's promises have been thoroughly tested and are guaranteed. God offers hope that will comfort and sustain you. In God's promises, you will find rest and renewal.

Now we will look at three promises that will help us fight the good fight of faith. You'll see how these promises address every one of our common struggles.

Promise # 1: God will never leave you nor forget you.

One of the greatest fears you can have is the fear of being alone. That's why challenges seem to be more intimidating when you are by yourself. It's why it can hurt so deeply when you are forgotten or abandoned. You weren't created to be alone, but to live in communion with God and others.

You can also feel alone when you experience great loss. It may be the death of a loved one or a shattered dream, but the heartache seems unbearable and the sense of isolation feels unnatural. You weren't created to experience death, injustice, evil, or the disease that can often lead to loss. In your sorrow, you can sometimes question God's justice, goodness, and purposes.

But in the face of your fears and sorrows, God has given you a great and precious promise. "He will never leave you nor forsake you" (Deuteronomy 31:6). In Isaiah 49, the people of Jerusalem complain that God has forgotten them. Listen to God's response: "Can a woman forget her nursing child, that she should have no compassion on the son of her womb? Even these may forget, yet I will not forget you. Behold, I have engraved you on the palms of my hands; your walls are continually before me" (vv. 15–16 ESV).

How can God forget you when he has engraved you on the palms of his hands? Jesus is perfect love, so in his presence you can live without fear. Jesus is the man of sorrows, acquainted with grief. He bore our grief and carried our sorrows (Isaiah 53:3–4). So, as you live in Christ, you can live with hope and rejoice in your salvation even in the midst of searing loss.

Promise # 2: Nothing can separate you from God's love.

In your shame, you can feel worthless and unlovable. In your guilt, you can wrestle with whether or not it's possible to forgive yourself. Your friends and family may reassure and affirm you, but somehow, you don't feel relief. The flashbacks and memories in your head convince you that you'll never be able to escape the traumatic memories. You may feel a sense of regret and you beat yourself up, wishing you could have responded differently.

Is there any good news in the midst of your shame and guilt? Paul declares the good news to us: "Who shall separate us from the love of Christ? Shall trouble or hardship or persecution or famine or nakedness or danger or sword? . . . No, in all these things we are more than conquerors through him who loved us. For I am convinced that neither death nor life, neither angels nor demons, neither the present nor the future, nor any powers, neither height nor depth, nor anything else in all creation, will be able to separate us from the love of God that is in Christ Jesus our Lord" (Romans 8:35, 37–39).

Your shame and guilt cannot separate you from God's love. God dealt with all of your reality through the cross of Jesus Christ. Jesus was shamed for you (Hebrews 12:2). He took your guilt and shame upon himself so you can live freely now before him. Moreover, Jesus suffered injustice and judgment so you can receive God's forgiveness, release your anger, and forgive others. Only God's promise of relentless love and forgiveness in Christ can transform your shame into confidence and joy and replace your guilt with humility and gratitude before God.

Promise # 3: God's love is better than life.

When we're in the midst of a struggle, we tend to reach out to people for help, to books to give us a better understanding, to food and drink for comfort, and to shows or video games as a way to escape. None of these things are inherently wrong. It's wise to seek counsel and do research before making a big decision. It's good to enjoy God's gifts and to rest. But do you tend to seek refuge in things you can see, taste, or touch more than finding refuge in your God? Are there times you are tempted to run away from reality to escape the difficulties of life or to satisfy the longings of your heart? This is the same sinful fantasy Adam and Eve indulged in the garden when they dreamed of a future apart from God's word and ways.

In the face of our fantasy, the Creator promises us that he is better than the tangible realities of life. He hasn't given us his good gifts in creation so we can serve those gifts, but so we might give thanks to him as the giver. Moreover, God knows that we most naturally understand life through concrete realities. That's why he uses stories and metaphors to communicate the reality of his goodness. Consider the way the psalmist delights in God:

> Because your love is better than life,
>   my lips will glorify you.
> I will praise you as long as I live,
>   and in your name I will lift up my hands.
> I will be fully satisfied as with the richest of foods;
>   with singing lips my mouth will praise you. (Psalm 63:3–5)

God uses tangible realities to point to the more glorious yet seemingly intangible reality of his love. God created your body and soul so that you not only experience his love, but you will know him personally and remember that he is the giver behind all of the good gifts. Only in him will you find your ultimate satisfaction and refuge. God wants to overwhelm you with his love and compel you by his love so that you will no longer live for yourself, but rather live for him.

RESPONSE ACTIVITIES (20 minutes)

Here is a selection of response questions and activities designed to stir your heart and soul and get you thinking deeply about the truths presented in this lesson. Write out your answers and reflections ahead of the group meeting, then be prepared to discuss your reflections together. **Consider your themes as you work through these questions.**

1. Broken promises can lead to broken trust. Think of a time when a family member or friend broke a promise. How did you respond?

2. What broken promises in your story may have led you to doubt and pull away from God?

3. Three big promises run throughout God's story: (1) God will never leave you nor forget you, (2) nothing can separate you from God's love, and (3) God's love is better than life. Which promise best helps you to know and experience God's love and deepens your trust in Christ?

4. Which promise is hardest for you to believe or receive? Share why. (As an exercise, take a moment to write out the promise that is hard to trust several times, writing "Amen" at the end. Then, say the promise aloud several times and say "amen" after each time. This is not a formula or mantra but rather a way of engaging God's Word with your senses as well as training yourself to trust in God's commitment to you.)

5. Storyboard: Reflect on what God has shown you in this lesson, and record it on the lesson 10 section of your storyboard in the back of the book (page 185).

READ AND ABIDE: PSALM 103
(15 minutes of personal reflection, followed by 20 minutes of group discussion)

1. **Understand your reality.** Open your heart to God before you open the Word of God. What is your battle with the Enemy like these days? You fight alongside God, so express to God how it is going.

2. **Look Up and See God's Reality.** Carefully read **Psalm 103**, which is about God and "all his benefits" (v. 2). Which of the benefits mentioned encourage you, and why? Note any verses that stand out to you. (For example: "Verse 4—He crowns me with his love and compassion.")

3. **Understand your heart struggle.** Most likely, the Enemy has made you wonder if some of these benefits really are true. Which of them does he cause you to doubt?

4. **Abide and rest in God.** Now read through Psalm 103 again, and this time pay close attention to what it says about the character of God—what kind of person he is. What does the psalm reveal about God's personality? How does this help you believe that his promised benefits really are true?

5. **Follow God's invitation.** Praise is the constant response in Psalm 103. How might you praise God in response, either with words or in your deeds?

LOOK AHEAD (5 minutes)

List 1–2 practical ways you will seek to live differently this week based on God's invitation. Share your ideas with the group.

PRAYER (5 minutes)

Close out your time responding to God through prayer, giving him thanks for his faithfulness and love that you have experienced during the lesson and small group time. Ask for his Spirit to empower you to put into practice what he is teaching you so you can live and love differently.

LESSON 11

REDEMPTION:

WE LIVE IN GOD'S POWER

BIG IDEA

Despite your weakness, and even *because* of your weakness, your life with God is a powerful life that experiences his love and bears fruit.

LOOK BACK (15 minutes)

Discuss among your group how God has enabled you to live differently, based on his invitation from the previous lesson's Read and Abide time.

THE BACKSTORY ON LIVING IN GOD'S POWER (10 minutes)

It doesn't take long for life to expose your limits, to show you that you are not in control. The longer you live, the more you experience brokenness in your own soul, struggles in your relationships, and the frailty of your body. Over time, you can grow weary and even begin to live a powerless life. God certainly gives you limitations. He didn't make you to conquer the world. But neither does he call you to merely survive.

Remember, God didn't just send the Son into the world to reconcile us to himself but also to restore us and enable us to live fully human lives. He has made it possible for you to be empowered by his Holy Spirit. He wants you to live a life where his strength is shown in your weakness, where you are able to know and experience his love, and where you bear the fruit of the Spirit's sanctifying work in and through your life.

Let's unpack each of these realities of an empowered life.

Empowered by the Holy Spirit

The same power God used to raise Jesus from the dead is at work in you and all of God's people—a power greater than all rule and authority in heaven and on earth (see Ephesians 1:19–21). God's power comes to you through your unbreakable union with Jesus Christ and through his Spirit, who will never leave you. Through your union with Christ, you are fully able to live an empowered Christian life. "His divine power has given us everything we need for a godly life through our knowledge of him who called us by his own glory and goodness. Through these he has given us his very great and precious promises, so that through them you may participate in the divine nature, having escaped the corruption in the world caused by evil desires" (2 Peter 1:3–4).

God's presence and God's promises are guaranteed through God's power. And we receive daily access to this power through our ongoing abiding with Christ. This is why Jesus said, "I am the vine; you are the branches. Whoever abides in me and I in him, he it is that bears much fruit, for apart from me you can do nothing" (John 15:5 ESV). A crucial theme in the gospel is that the only way you can live *for* God is to live *with* God. We can live with God because he has given us his Spirit. Just as your union with Jesus Christ is not merely a theological concept but a life-giving reality to be known and experienced, God's power is not some abstract superhero power found only in comic books but a supernatural reality we can access by daily seeking communion with God through his Spirit, who already dwells within us: "For the Kingdom of God is not just a lot of talk; it is living by God's power" (1 Corinthians 4:20 NLT). "For this reason, I remind you to fan into flame the gift of God, which is in you. . . . For God gave us a spirit not of fear but of power and love and self-control" (2 Timothy 1:6–7 ESV).

Empowered in Your Weakness

Jesus brought you into union with himself so you can experience his power in your weakness. God knows all the struggles you face in this fallen world. He hears your tearful prayers as you plead with him to calm your fears and he is with you in the midst of your deep shame. He knows how you doubt his goodness and power in ways that have led not only to despair but also a growing distance from him. He has seen your heart harden as you have grown angry and bitter in disappointment and discouragement. Jesus lived and walked in the midst of all the realities of the fall. He experienced all the pain, testing, and temptation you face in this world. But he lived with power. And Jesus lived, died, and rose again so that you, and all of God's people, can live with power as well: "For to be sure, he was crucified in weakness, yet he lives by God's power. Likewise, we are weak in him, yet by God's power we will live with him in our dealing with you" (2 Corinthians 13:4–5).

Just as he did for Paul, God will meet you with his power in your weakness. Take the words of 2 Corinthians 12:9–10, where Paul boasts of his weakness, and hear them as if God were speaking directly to you. They would go something like this: "My grace is sufficient for you, for my power is made perfect in weakness. Therefore, boast all the more gladly about your weaknesses, so that my power may rest on you. That is why, for my sake, you delight in your weaknesses, in your insults, in your hardships, in your persecutions, in your difficulties. For when you are weak, then I am strong."

God invites you to know Christ in your struggles and to experience the power of his resurrected life even in the midst of life's storms. As you draw near and hold fast to Jesus, you can fellowship with him in your suffering as God conforms you more and more to Christ's image. You see, God takes what is intended for evil and uses it for good. In ways that are hard to explain, you realize that God's power is coursing through your soul as you experience contentment in your weakness, confidence in your hardships, and comfort in the chaos.

With the Holy Spirit's help and in the midst of your weakness, you can live with God's power in at least two distinct ways: (1) by knowing and experiencing his love, and (2) by bearing the fruit of good works.

Empowered to Know and Experience His Love

You were created for love—to be loved and to love. So why does love seems so elusive, so hard to find, and even harder to keep? The **flesh** seeks to convince you that love is a feeling that revolves around your interests and needs. The **world** sends the message that you deserve to be happy and you should get what you want. The **devil** seeks to undermine how you know and experience God's love, and tries to convince you that God and others need to serve you instead of the other way around. But the evil trinity's tactics are mind games and smokescreens that can't hold up to the piercing reality of our God, who *is* love.

You see, God not only declared his love for us but also demonstrated his love through Jesus's death on the cross. There is no greater love than the Father sending his Son to die in our place and to bring us, his adulterous people, back into an unbreakable covenant relationship with himself. God poured out his love into our hearts through his Spirit so we can abide in his love and be perfected by his love.

God wants you to enjoy and experience the fullness of his love. Paul's prayer summarizes God's heart: "I pray that out of his glorious riches he may strengthen you with power through his Spirit in your inner being, so that Christ may dwell in your hearts through faith. And I pray that you, being rooted and established in love, may have power, together with all the Lord's holy people, to grasp how wide and long and high and deep is the love of Christ, and to know this love that surpasses knowledge—that you may be filled to the measure of all the fullness of God" (Ephesians 3:16–19).

God's love not only grounds you in the storms of life, but also compels you to no longer live for yourself, but for Jesus, who loved you and gave himself for you. Knowing and experiencing God's love shapes how you live and what you live for.

God's Power Bears Fruit

As we live with God and live for God, the Spirit bears fruit in us as we abide in the love of Christ. God's Spirit fills us with "love, joy, peace, patience, kindness, goodness, faithfulness, gentleness, self-control" (Galatians 5:22–23 esv). Such fruit helps us to thrive even in the worst of times. Have you witnessed the peace and joy of a loved one who is facing a terminal illness? Have you talked with a quadriplegic who not only endures with hope but also proclaims the hope found in Jesus in the face of decades of excruciating chronic pain? Have you seen the kind of undeniable peace that empowers a person to give thanks to God even when their marriage is not what they dreamed of or when their child goes astray?

Such fruit is an amazing gift! It's not something to be achieved by a few based on pedigree or performance. No, God created and redeemed all of his people to enjoy a fruitful life through communion with Christ—by receiving, praying, and living his word through the power of his Spirit. As we abide in Christ, God's power changes our thoughts, emotions, and desires. He deepens our faith, fuels our hope, and compels us by his love to live for him and not for ourselves. This life of renewal drives us to participate in his mission, living a life of love for our neighbor both in the church and in the world. "May the God of hope fill you with all joy and peace as you trust in him, so that you may overflow with hope by the power of the Holy Spirit" (Romans 15:13).

RESPONSE ACTIVITIES (20 minutes)

Here is a selection of response questions and activities designed to stir your heart and soul and get you thinking deeply about the truths presented in this lesson. Write out your answers and reflections ahead of the group meeting, then be prepared to discuss your reflections together. **Consider your themes as you work through these questions.**

1. Where on the spectrum do you tend to live as you face your weakness: (1) lingering in your brokenness as you live a "powerless" life, or (2) relying on your own strength as you seek control and strive for success?

2. How has God shown his power toward you in the midst of your weaknesses? How does God's power in you enable you to see your weaknesses differently?

3. How does Jesus make it possible for you to boast in your weakness?

4. Review the Bible passages in this lesson. They are intended to highlight what God's power can accomplish in your life and in the lives of all of God's people as we abide in him. Which passage comforts you the most? Share why. Which passages build your trust and confidence in God and his power? Share why.

5. Storyboard: Take a moment to reflect on what you've learned about living in God's power, and then fill out your storyboard thoughts on this lesson in the back of the book (page 185).

READ AND ABIDE: PSALM 46
(15 minutes of personal reflection, followed by 20 minutes of group discussion)

1. **Understand Your reality.** Open your heart to God before you open the Word of God. In what ways do you feel weak or unable? Begin by telling it to the God of all power.

2. **Look up and see God's reality.** Read **Psalm 46** slowly one or two times. What are some defining characteristics of God's power? Note any verses that stand out to you. (For example: "Verse 1—God's power is an always present help in my troubles.")

3. **Understand your heart struggles.** How well do you accept the truth that you can be weak because your God is strong? In what parts of your life do you find it hard to trust God, either by sitting in your brokenness or by preferring to trust your own strength?

4. Abide and rest in God. The psalm speaks of God's control of all things today, and also (in verses 8–10) of the coming day when he will completely end all troubles. How does it help you to know that both are true?

5. Follow God's invitation. With the promises that (1) God holds all power today and (2) he will be fully exalted among the nations one day, what might you dare to do for God that would be too scary otherwise?

LOOK AHEAD (5 minutes)

List 1–2 practical ways you will seek to live differently this week based on God's invitation. Share your ideas with the group.

PRAYER (5 minutes)

Close out your time responding to God through prayer, giving him thanks for his faithfulness and love that you have experienced during the lesson and small group time. Ask for his Spirit to empower you to put into practice what he is teaching you so you can live and love differently.

LESSON 12
CONSUMMATION:
WE WILL ENJOY LOVE FOREVER

BIG IDEA

Your story will join with God's story even more perfectly one day when your body and soul, the world you live in, and the love you share with God are all made new.

LOOK BACK (15 minutes)

Discuss among your group how God has enabled you to live differently, based on his invitation from the previous lesson's Read and Abide time.

THE BACKSTORY ON OUR FUTURE LIFE (10 minutes—Read aloud in group.)

I hope your journey through *Restore* has been fruitful, helping you see how God's story gives meaning and hope to your own story. God's story is so much more than a history book that narrates what took place between two time periods. Rather, God's story reveals a living reality about Jesus, the Son of God, who created all things, who holds all things together, and who declares, "I am making everything new" (Revelation 21:5). Though we live in the middle of God's story and have not yet reached the end, even now God reveals to us what is yet to come. Every day, we catch glimpses of what our end will be like: breathtaking sunsets, moments of peace and calm, a sense of comfort from spending time in God's Word, a wonderful meal with close friends, or a sense of life-giving purpose as we work, serve, and play. One day, beauty and joy won't be confined to such moments. We will experience this and more forever and ever.

An End That Is a Beginning

As a Christian, you are united with Christ. Nothing can change that, not even death. In fact, your physical death will allow you to experience your relationship with God in a whole new way.

First, the unfolding story of redemption not only gives hope for our souls but also offers redemption for our broken bodies. One day, God will **transform our natural bodies into resurrected bodies**. "The body that is sown is perishable, it is raised imperishable; it is sown in dishonor, it is raised in glory; it is sown in weakness, it is raised in power; it is sown a natural body, it is raised a spiritual body" (1 Corinthians 15:42–44). Our supernatural bodies will be free from disease, disorder, deformities, and limitations, enabling us to experience love, joy, and peace in infinitely greater and more profound ways.

Second, God will not only one day glorify our bodies, he will also **fully unite God's people to Jesus in perfect communion**. When heaven is depicted on television or in movies, you often hear about the streets paved with gold or the pearly gates. But what do you see as you look at this passage?

> Then I saw a new heaven and a new earth, for the first heaven and the first earth had passed away, and there was no longer any sea. I saw the Holy City, the new Jerusalem, coming down out of heaven from God, prepared as a bride beautifully dressed for her husband. And I heard a loud voice from the throne saying, "Look! God's dwelling place is now among the people, and he will dwell with them. They will be his people, and God himself will be with them and be their God." (Revelation 21:1–3)

Here we see the Holy City, but the vision quickly shifts to a holy bride, beautifully dressed for her husband. At the beginning of God's story in the Old Testament, he described his promise of redemption in terms of a future marriage. Now here, in the last chapter of God's story, you see God fulfilling his covenant promise when Jesus Christ consummates his marriage to his bride, the church.

Another significant reality we can't afford to miss is how the writer wants us to look and listen to the ultimate reality in the age to come.

God "will dwell with them. They will be his people, and God himself will be with them and be their God." We "will dwell in the house of the LORD forever" (Psalm 23:6).

It's also important to see and understand what will be absent in the new heaven and earth. "He will wipe every tear from their eyes. There will be no more death or mourning or crying or pain, for the old order of things has passed away. He who was seated on the throne said, 'I am making everything new!' Then he said, '"Write this down, for these words are trustworthy and true"' (Revelation 21:4–5).

Imagine living where there is no more harm, no more sickness, no more danger, no more death. Imagine a perfect peace where there are no stressors within you or around you.

This wondrous vision does not end here. It continues to unfold in greater detail and beauty, showing us what it will mean to truly dwell with God. "No longer will there be any curse. The throne of God and of the Lamb will be in the city, and his servants will serve him. They will see his face, and his name will be on their foreheads. There will be no more night. They will not need the light of a lamp or the light of the sun, for the Lord God will give them light. And they will reign for ever and ever" (Revelation 22:3–5).

One day, there will no longer be any curse. No more temptation. No more darkness. You will be set free from horrific memories and emotions from the past. "The former things will not be remembered, nor will they come to mind" (Isaiah 65:17). You will no longer have any knowledge or exposure to evil, only to good. All the work of redemption done in the crucible of suffering and sin will be complete. You will work, rest, relax, and enjoy life without struggle.

Living in Perfect Communion with God

The very communion we were created to have with God will finally be experienced perfectly and eternally. Let's imagine what that communion will be like.

We will know God perfectly, without any distortion or deficit. We will no longer need eyes of faith because "then we shall see face to face" (1 Corinthians 13:11–12). We will know his glory more fully, such that

God's glory will be our glory and our glory will be God's glory. We will know the height, depth, width, and breadth of God's love personally, because we will no longer battle any faith struggles.

Furthermore, **we will experience God's presence** and power in every fiber of our being. Seeing and experiencing God's glory will bring lasting change to our bodies and souls. In glory, there will no longer be any crevasse of selfishness or sinfulness in our hearts and minds. Experiencing God's perfect, life-sustaining love will obliterate any fantasy for something more or different from God. We will no longer experience any form of anger since we will experience perfect unity and peace with God and others in a place that is free of disaster, disease, and death. Because there will be no more loss of any kind, there will be no more sorrow. We will experience love, joy, and peace in ways that will satisfy our souls beyond measure, and as a result, we will never again struggle with fear, shame, or guilt. We will no longer deal with any common struggles.

Finally, **we will image God** perfectly since we will relate and respond to him without sin. God's love will fully rule our hearts so that we will relate to God totally out of a desire to please him, no longer tempted to live for ourselves. We will **relate** to others in ways motivated purely by love for God and love for them, where we consider them more important than ourselves. We will **respond** to God with perfect submission, which will result in perfect obedience through the power of God's Spirit. We will also **respond** to others exactly how God responds to each of us— with patience, kindness, goodness, faithfulness, gentleness, and self-control. We will longer experience the pain of relational struggles.

Consummation brings complete restoration. Finally, your story will be completely redeemed by and aligned with God's story. More than ever, we can rejoice always, pray without ceasing, and give thanks in all circumstances. No fairy tale can compare to such an ending that marks the beginning of a never-ending life of love.

You Don't Have to Wait

In many ways, you already have the privilege of living now how you will live forever. You can enjoy now what you will enjoy forever. The same God who makes consummation a reality is with you now. The same God who will wipe away every tear is already now the God "who comforts us in all our troubles" (2 Corinthians 1:3–4). You don't have to wait until heaven to know God and to be changed by his unfailing love and glory. You don't have to wait until heaven to experience God's presence, promises, and power. You have full access now to your everlasting God through your union with Christ. God invites you to live fully in his story so that it can transform every aspect of your story.

Right now, you may think your struggles will never end and you can't imagine your future could be so beautiful. But on this journey, God is restoring your soul and redeeming your story with every step and with every glimpse of Jesus. *Someday, your journey through brokenness will end.* You will be fully formed in Christ—formed by his glory and for his glory. In the meantime, enjoy and respond to your Father's love. Draw near to the Son, who gives you rest. Be courageous and strong through the Spirit, so you don't grow weary and lose heart.

Let's close with a final invitation from Jesus to abide in him until the end:

> "I am the Alpha and the Omega, the First and the Last, the Beginning and the End. . . .
>
> "I, Jesus, have sent my angel to give you this testimony for the churches. I am the Root and the Offspring of David, and the bright Morning Star."
>
> The Spirit and the bride say, "Come!" And let the one who hears say, "Come!" Let the one who is thirsty come; and let the one who wishes take the free gift of the water of life." (Revelation 22:13–17)

RESPONSE ACTIVITIES (20 minutes)

Here is a selection of response questions and activities designed to stir your heart and soul and get you thinking deeply about the truths presented in this lesson. Write out your answers and reflections ahead of the group meeting, then be prepared to discuss your reflections together. **Consider your themes as you work through these questions.**

1. In this lesson, we reviewed some of the consummation realities that we will experience in the new heaven and earth. In light of your story and struggles, which future realities are hardest for you to receive? List them out.

2. Take a moment to read through Revelation 21:1–15 and 22–27. Make a few lists described below, and then reflect.

List the future realities of which "there will be no more . . ."

List the future realities in which "there will be perfect . . ."

1 Corinthians 13:12 says, "Now I know in part; then I shall know fully." List the future realities you can experience in part now.

How does knowing these future realities are coming help you live differently now?

3. Storyboard: Complete your storyboard at the back of the book on page 185. Add reflections from this lesson, and also sum up some ways these lessons and the storyboard have helped you see how God is redeeming your story.

READ AND ABIDE: REVELATION 21:1–8, 22–27
(15 minutes of personal reflection, followed by 20 minutes of group discussion)

1. Understand your reality. Open your heart to God before you open the Word of God. Consider your weak body, your still-sinning heart, and your trouble-filled world. What do you especially long for God to make new? Tell him about it.

2. Look up and see God's reality. Read **Revelation 21:1–8 and 22–27** again. What aspects of the new heaven and new earth do you most look forward to, and why? Note any verses that stand out to you. (For example: "Verse 3—dwelling with God and he with me.")

3. Understand your heart struggles. What keeps this vision of the future from being the great hope of your life and the expectation that drives all you do? It might be:
• You're not sure this future will actually happen.

- You're not really captivated by the truth that having such intimacy with God will bring you perfect joy.
- It's hard to keep unseen glories in mind when the troubles you see every day feel more real and pressing.
- God's work in you feels slow (or missing) much of the time, so it's hard to believe he has such a glorious plan for you.
- Something else.

Write a few sentences that explain your struggle to live with heaven-focused hope.

4. **Abide and rest in God.** Meditate for several minutes on God's promise in verse 5: "I am making everything new." What hope do these words give you?

5. Follow God's invitation. How might you feel freed up to love God and others when you have confidence that this vision is your eternal future? How might you live today? What might you do?

LOOK AHEAD (5 minutes)

List 1–2 practical ways you will seek to live differently this week based on God's invitation. Share your ideas with the group.

PRAYER (5 minutes)

Close out your time responding to God through prayer, giving him thanks for his faithfulness and love that you have experienced during the lesson and small group time. Ask for his Spirit to empower you to put into practice what he is teaching you so you can live and love differently.

LESSON 13
REFLECTION, NEXT STEPS, AND TESTIMONY

BIG IDEA

As you look back on your journey, you may be surprised how God has been reframing how you see life, restoring your soul broken by evil, and redeeming your story marked by heartache.

LOOK BACK (15 minutes)

Discuss among your group how God has enabled you to live differently, based on his invitation from the previous lesson's Read and Abide time.

THE BACKSTORY ON WHAT IT MEANS FOR JESUS TO RESTORE OUR SOULS (10 minutes—Read aloud in group.)

When Jesus, our Good Shepherd, restores our souls (Psalm 23:3), it doesn't mean that all of the ways evil has hurt and disordered our souls has been removed or "fixed." Though evil and sin remain within and around us—continually deforming the way we think, feel, live, and love—God nevertheless is also continuously at work to restore our souls. As Paul writes, "our inner person is being renewed day by day" (2 Corinthians 4:16 csb). So, what does it mean for God to renew and restore our souls on an ongoing basis?

We know that Jesus is restoring our souls whenever our thoughts, emotions, and desires align with his. Our souls are restored in the midst of anxiety as our minds learn to dwell on Christ's reassuring promises. We're restored when we learn to trust and embrace his truth in the midst of our confusion and even our sin. After David committed adultery and murder, God's Spirit brought him to repentance and prompted him to cry out, "Restore to me the joy of your salvation and grant me a willing spirit, to sustain me" (Psalm 51:12). Our Comforter binds up our broken hearts when we experience his presence in our loneliness, his comfort in our pain, and his acceptance in our shame. He renews our inner being as we learn to desire his love more than the objects of our lusts and when we long to be in his presence in the face of our fears.

We know that Jesus is restoring our souls when his Spirit empowers us to live and love in ways that reflect him. His love is perfected in us as we forgive those who have deeply hurt us, and as we love others in relational and practical ways during their time of need. He revives our souls as we rejoice, as we pray, and as we give thanks in Christ. He matures our souls as we live with unexplainable contentment and joy in our chronic pain or unchanging circumstances. He restores our souls as we live by faith, clinging to him in obedience while everything within and around us is pulling us toward evil. In other words, we know that Jesus is restoring our souls whenever we live in the Spirit and not in the flesh (see Galatians 5:13–26). Jesus renews our souls as we are compelled by his love to live for him and not for ourselves. Jesus revives our souls as the beauty and glory of God outweigh the darkness and pain in our hearts, allowing us to rest and live with a hope that surpasses understanding.

In the new heavens and earth, when we dwell in the very presence of God, our souls, as well as our bodies, will be fully restored because evil will be destroyed. Because our bodies and souls will be wholly redeemed, the flashbacks, trigger points, and any other adverse responses to evil will be wiped away. As the prophet Isaiah declared, "The former things will not be remembered, nor will they come to mind" (Isaiah 65:17). Instead, in the absence of evil we will experience the fullness of God's presence, and we will be radiant as we bask in his overwhelming glory and love.

RESPONSE ACTIVITY (10 minutes per person)

You may have been hesitant to work through or share your story. Perhaps your focus was on your struggles or how the issues of others were your biggest problems. Through the weeks of *Restore*, we pray you not only have become more aware of Christ in your story, but also have been spending more time abiding in him through his Word. Now that you are at the end of *Restore*, God may have helped you reframe how you see all of life, including your relationship with him and others. You may have experienced moments, or even a season, of the restoring work of God's love, peace, and joy in your soul. You may be at a point where you see how God is redeeming your story, where he has taken what was meant for evil and is using it for your good and his glory. You may even be at a place where you now see your story as God's story so that when you share your story with others, it's more about God's faithfulness and love than about you and your struggles. Regardless of where you are in your journey, God is still working in you, and he will be with you always. His love will pursue you all the days of your life.

Reflection

Take a moment and look at your Look Back journaling activity at the beginning of Lesson 1 (page 15) so you can remember where you were at and what you were experiencing before you started. Also look through your storyboard (pages 183) to see how God has been reframing how you see your life and struggles, as well as how you see him and others, and how God has been restoring your soul.

After reviewing and reflecting on these two sections, you can use the following chart to look back at how you would have described your life before and after *Restore*. There is much that may still feel unresolved or that you're just now beginning to understand. That's okay. God is not looking to tie up your story and struggles with a pretty bow. Instead, God wants to shift your perspective, stir your affections for him, and change how you relate and respond to him and others—with growing freedom, love, and joy. The goal here is testify to what God has done in and around you during your time in *Restore* and how he is calling you to live and love differently. For the "After *Restore*" column, consider how using God's story as a framework helped you see and understand life differently.

Before *Restore*	**After** *Restore*
How I saw and understood my story, struggles, and themes.	How God's story helps me to see and understand my story, struggles, and themes differently.
How I saw and understood God and how I related to him.	How God's story helps me to see and understand him and how that changes how I relate to him.
How I experienced my struggles in my body and soul (heart).	How I experience my God in my body and soul (heart).
How I expected God to help and heal me.	How I experience God restoring my soul.
How I saw and understood others and how I related to them.	How I see and understand others and how I relate to them.

Next Steps

As you have seen throughout each movement of his story, God invites you to enjoy life with him. God's Spirit is always at work, helping you remember his presence, promises, and power. He's inviting you to come to him for rest and to respond to his love by trusting and obeying him each moment of every day. What are some next steps that God may be calling you to take? In light of his story, how has he encouraged you to live differently? Before looking over the list of possibilities below, ask God to show you specific areas where he is calling you to step out in faith.

Option #1: Share your story with others. Now that you have taken the time to work through your themes based on the experiences in your life, you might seek out a trusted friend or two and tell them your story. You might be afraid to tell others your story because you're ashamed or guilty, or because you worry what others may think or say. If this is the case, remember that your story is not ultimately about you. It's the story of God's faithfulness to redeem your reality by the power of his gospel.

Option #2: Rethink your identity. God's story not only shapes your story but also your identity. How might God want to change the way you see yourself? How might a renewed understanding that you are created in the image of God and that you are in union with Christ reshape your living and loving?

Option #3: Seek to reconcile or restore a relationship. First, consider how you might restore your communion with God. Confess ways you've sinned and failed to love him and others. Whatever distance you have placed between yourself and God, he will not let anything separate you from his love. Next, ask God to show you other relationships in your life that could be restored or deepened. Are there any relationships with old friends or family members that need to be reconciled? Are there any relationships you can seek to deepen, such as those with a parent, spouse, child, neighbor, or coworker? As you reflect on how God has restored his relationship with you, consider how you can share God's healing love with others.

Option #4: Forgive and seek forgiveness. Through the process of *Restore*, you may have become more aware of how you have hurt others or how others have hurt you. God's love covers the worst of sins, and his forgiveness cleanses the worst of sinners. Meditate on how much God has forgiven you. Rejoice and give thanks for his undeserved mercy and grace. In response, humble yourself and ask those you have hurt to forgive you. If you've also been sinned against, forgive those who have hurt you. Forgiveness frees you to live the life of love God intends.

Option #5: Work through more of your story. Are there more areas of your life where you struggle to see God? Are there more areas of weakness where you want to find strength? Bring these longings and questions to God, perhaps by working through the activity in lesson 2 again.

Option #6: Invite others to take this journey. Sometimes we don't know the people closest to us as well as we could or ought. Now that you have experienced how God redeems your story in ways that bring healing and growth, and how he restores your soul in ways that free you to love God and others, pray about who you would like to invite to take this journey with you. Who seems to be overwhelmed by life or defined by their story, or who just desires to grow as a disciple of Jesus Christ? Consider those in your neighborhood, accountability group, workplace, or church. Regardless of who it is, you can be confident that God will do his beautiful redeeming work through Christ by the power of his Spirit.

Prepare a *Restore* Testimony

> Give thanks to the LORD, for he is good;
>   his love endures forever.
> Let the redeemed of the LORD tell their story. (Psalm 107:1–2)

One of the most effective ways of giving God glory is by testifying to his power and love. God uses testimonies to encourage others to draw near to him through his story.

Life with God involves praise to God for his unfailing and redeeming love. As a way to testify to God's goodness and faithfulness, please take some time to reflect and respond to the following questions, which serve as a guide in crafting your testimony as you share your story within God's story. As you answer these questions, take a look back through your *Restore* storyboard or your journal.

The Four Parts of Your *Restore* Testimony

Part One: Your Story (about a paragraph)

Consider what your life was like prior to participating in *Restore*. Think about how you were living and loving.

- How did the fall impact how you saw and understood your **life** and **relationships**? What were some resultant **themes** in your story?
- How did the fall impact how you **related to and experienced God**?

Part Two: Reframing How You See All Things (about a paragraph)

Think about how learning and understanding God's story has enabled you to reframe the way you view your own story.

- How does God's story change the way you see **your story** and **struggles**?
- How does God's story change the way you see **God** and **his relationship with you**?

Part Three: Restoring Your Soul (about two paragraphs)

God uses his story to **restore** us. Jesus restores our souls when he aligns our thoughts, emotions, and desires with his. Jesus restores us as we abide in this love through his Word and receive his comfort and peace. Jesus restores us by helping us to trust his promises and embrace him even in the midst of fear and confusion. Although our souls will not be completely restored until heaven, think about how God has been at work in you.

- How has God been restoring your soul and body through **his Spirit**?
- How has God used **God's people** to help restore your soul?
- What specific passages in **God's Word** have helped you to know and experience his love?

Part Four: Living and Loving Differently (about a paragraph)

In response to how God is reframing how you see and understand life and how he is restoring your soul, share how you are living more in his story.

- How is God calling you to **live** differently?
- How is God calling you to **love** those in your life differently?

Thank you for prayerfully writing out and sharing your testimony so that God will be glorified and more people will know and experience God through his story.

READ AND ABIDE

The pattern of questions used in this book's Read and Abide exercises can be used for any passage of Scripture. I encourage you to use these five steps during your personal Scripture reading.

1. **Understand your reality.** Before you open the Word of God, open your heart to God. What part of your story or reality feels overwhelming or painful right now?
2. **Look up and see God's reality**. Read the passage slowly one or two times. Note what truths it reveals about God and his love for you. Note any verses that stand out to you.
3. **Understand your heart struggles**. How is your heart struggling to receive these truths? How do your story and struggles keep you living "under the clouds"?
4. **Abide and rest in God**. How does this passage address your story and reality, helping you to know and experience the love and comfort of Christ through the clouds?
5. **Follow God's invitation.** How is God calling you to trust and obey him right now so that you can love him and others in Christ?

LOOK AHEAD (5 minutes)

List 1–2 practical ways you will seek to live differently this week based on God's invitation. Share your ideas with the group.

PRAYER (5 minutes)

Close out your time responding to God through prayer, giving him thanks for his faithfulness and love that you have experienced during this study and small group time. Ask for his Spirit to empower you to put into practice what he is teaching you so you can live and love differently.

GLOSSARY OF TERMS

THE FOLLOWING terms are defined according to the way they are used in the *Restore* material. Know that these terms sometimes have a broader range of meaning outside of this context.

STORY

God's story. The Bible's account of the reality of God's loving and redeeming work in Jesus Christ. God's story unfolds in four big movements:

- *Creation* shows how God created us for love.
- *The fall* shows how evil keeps us from love.
- *Redemption* shows how Jesus restores us with love.
- *Consummation* shows how we will enjoy love forever.

reference point. An established reality or set of values you use to compare, understand, and respond to your life experiences.

reframe. To reinterpret how you see and understand your reality in accordance with God's reality as it's revealed through his word.

theme. In your story, a big idea or takeaway message you would use to describe how you experienced certain impactful life moments. In God's story, a big idea or takeaway message that describes who God is or what he does throughout the history of his redemptive work.

your story. An account of the realities of your life that highlights the relationships and experiences that have impacted you. Your story is not independent of, but rather included in, God's story.

CREATION

body and soul. Our integrated being. God created us with a body (our outward, physical being) and a soul (our inward, spiritual being). These are integrated such that what impacts one impacts the other.

emotions. An experience of what we value and believe. These are more than simply impulses. Our intertwined thoughts and emotions produce desires and inclinations, which in turn affect and energize how we respond.

God's commands. The way God has created and presently calls us to live, as well as how we shouldn't live. Obeying God's commands leads to life; turning away from his commands (sin) leads to death (Psalm 19; 119; John 15:9–11; Romans 5:20).

heart. A biblical term used interchangeably with *soul* to describe the essence of our inner, spiritual being through which we relate and respond to life. Our heart experiences and responds to life situations practically through *thoughts, emotions,* and *desires* (TED).

image of God. A description of how God created us to reflect him in the way we relate and respond to him and others. We image God as we love him and others.

THE FALL

common struggles. The ways our hearts respond to evil. These are not simply passive responses, but can also be active responses informed by our thoughts, emotions, and desires.

- *Fantasy* is refusing to accept or address your actual situation, instead seeking a different reality that offers an imagined escape or hope.
- *Guilt* is pain that comes from with something you've done wrong.
- *Shame* is pain that comes from who you are or who you think you are.

- *Fear* is an anxious anticipation of something perceived to be threatening or dangerous.
- *Anger* is a strong feeling of displeasure or hostility in response to something or someone that opposes what you value.
- *Sorrow* is deep sadness or despair, usually resulting from loss.

evil trinity. The world, our sinful flesh, and the devil (1 John 2:16).

faith struggles. A way of describing our battle to believe and hope in Christ. Faith struggles usually involve questioning God's love. Such struggles include doubts, despair, and a sense of distance in our relationship with God.

flesh. Our sinful human nature (Romans 7:17). At the core of our sinful nature is our bent towards self-love and self-glory (Romans 1:21–23; 2 Timothy 3:1–5).

heart struggles. A way to describe how our soul struggles as we live in this fallen world. Our heart struggles include common struggles, relational struggles, and faith struggles.

relational struggles. A way of describing the difficulties we face loving God and others. They include our failures to love and also how others fail to love us.

schemes of the Enemy. Attempts by the devil to undermine our relationship with God and others in four common ways: he deceives (John 8:44), distracts (Matthew 13:20–22), discourages (Joshua 1:9–11; Hebrews 12:3), and divides (Ephesians 4:3–6).

sin. Both a condition due to our nature, and an action of rejecting God, despising his Word, and doing evil in his sight (Romans 7:18; 1 Samuel 8:7; 2 Samuel 12:9).

spiritual warfare. The relentless battle between the kingdom of God and the kingdom of evil. Through his various schemes, the Enemy seeks to undermine our knowledge and experience of God's love (Ephesians 6:10–17).

struggles. A way to describe how we sin and suffer in a fallen world. In our sin, we suffer since we are not living as God created us to live. In our suffering, we can sin as we battle to trust and obey God.

temptation. Not necessarily sin, but rather an invitation to turn away from God and towards evil (James 1:14).

test. An invitation to trust and obey God. God tests us, but he never tempts us toward evil (James 1:13).

trials. Both temptations and tests (James 1:12).

REDEMPTION

abide in Christ. The means through which we can experience a more intimate communion with God. We abide in Christ when we receive, pray, and obey his Word by faith and through the power of his Spirit. (John 15:1–17; Galatians 5:13–26)

communion with God. How we experience our relationship with God (John 17:20–26; 1 John 1:3). Because we live in a fallen world, the sense of closeness in our fellowship with God ebbs and flows like the ocean tides.

faith. A confidence in who Jesus is and the conviction that he has the power to do what he promised (Hebrews 11:1; Romans 4:21).

repentance. Turning away from evil and returning to God in trust and obedience.

union with Christ. The intimate, covenant relationship God established for us through Christ in salvation. Our union with Christ is steadfast and never changes (Galatians 2:20; 17:20–23)

CONSUMMATION

absence of evil. All evil wiped away; consequently, all sin and death, along with all of our struggles (common, relational, faith) existing no more (Revelation 21:4; 27; 22:3).

glorified bodies. Resurrected, spiritual bodies that are transformed and made imperishable and immortal, raised in glory and power in Christ (1 Corinthians 15:42–44).

new heaven and earth. Another biblical description of consummation, marked by the return of Christ when he makes all things new and brings about complete restoration (Revelation 21:5).

presence of God. The coming experience in which we will dwell in perfect communion with God. There will be no need for the sun or moon because God's glory will illuminate the heavens and the earth (Revelation 21:3). It will be as evident as the noonday sun, and we will no longer live under the clouds of sin and death (Proverbs 4:18).

LEADER'S NOTES

I AM excited you have the opportunity to disciple and care for God's people by journeying through *Restore*. This guide can be used in a range of small group contexts, from discipleship groups or community groups to classes within the local church. Use the portion of the guide that's relevant for your particular context. Plan on at least thirteen sessions to get through the material in *Restore*. Each participant should have their own workbook and should work through each lesson on their own before the group meets to discuss it.

As a leader, keep in mind the following **good news** for you as a person providing discipleship and care in community.

1. **You can be confident in Christ**. You shouldn't be confident in yourself, but only in Christ. God uses you by his grace to build up his body in love and to advance his kingdom despite your shortcomings. Christ is the sufficient One who makes you sufficient by his Spirit (2 Corinthians 3:4–6).

2. **You can relax—the pressure is off**. You can't fix anyone. You can't change anyone's circumstances, let alone their heart. So, you don't have to ask perfect questions or say just the right truth for God to do his redeeming work. God is actively at work to complete what he began (Philippians 1:6).

3. **You can be gentle and loving**. God calls you to speak the truth in love (Ephesians 4:15). You can't convict anyone with harsh words. You can't make participants see their reality more clearly. But God's kindness leads to repentance as his Spirit convicts, reveals, and softens hearts (Romans 2:4).

4. **You can be patient**. You can't force things to happen. You can't orchestrate a timetable or help someone "get it" or grow faster.

You shouldn't make assumptions or jump to conclusions before drawing out their hearts. God works before, during, and even after your group time. God's timing is his own, but you can trust him.

5. **You can work hard**. You aren't on a vacation. You live in the midst of a spiritual battle. Ministry is hard, and spiritual warfare is relentless, but God's energy and power works within you (Ephesians 6:10–20; Colossians 1:29).

6. **You can rely on others**. You can't bear burdens alone and you don't need to have all of the answers. Some of the most helpful questions and answers may come from participants in your group. When that happens, don't feel discouraged that you didn't think to ask that great question or provide the response yourself, but praise God for how he works through all his people.

7. **You can walk alongside others**. You are together on the same journey. No one has arrived. You are not the dispenser of grace. Rather, all of us are receiving God's grace.

NOTES FOR EACH LESSON

The following guide highlights key areas for you to be aware of, clarify, or address as needed as you work through each lesson.

- The Response Activity questions at the end of each lesson do not have a right or wrong answer. They are meant to help group participants (1) reflect about their reality in light of God's reality, (2) apply God's truth to their lives, (3) share reflections with one another so that participants encourage each other, and (4) draw near to Christ through his Word.

- Encourage those in your group to take a moment each week to take some time filling out the storyboard at the back of the book (page 183–185), writing how God is **reframing** how they see their life and relationships and how he is **restoring** their soul. If they capture how God is at work through each lesson, they will be able to see the subtle and significant ways God is **redeeming** their story over the course of their journey.

General Weekly Schedule

Here is a helpful schedule for shepherding those in your group during your hour and a half meeting time. You can find the more detailed description for each section on page 8 ("What to Expect in Each Lesson").

- **Look Back** (15 minutes)—to discuss how God enabled the participants to live differently, based on God's invitation from the previous week's Read and Abide time.
- **Backstory** (10 minutes)—to read the lesson out loud in the group.
- **Response Activity** (20 minutes)—to share reflections from the Response Activity questions.
- **Read and Abide** (35 minutes total: 15 minutes of personal reflection, followed by 20 minutes of group discussion)
- **Look Ahead** (5 minutes)— Each person will share how they will seek to live differently during the coming week based on God's invitation from the Read and Abide time.
- **Pray** (5 minutes)—close out the group with a brief prayer time. Seek to end by the agreed upon time in order to respect everyone's time.

General Schedule for Sharing Stories (Lesson 2)

- **Small Group Guidelines** (5 minutes)—During the first week of sharing stories, read through the entire guide (at the end of Lesson 2) by asking people to read one tip out loud as you go around the group. The guidelines will help people to know how to listen to and encourage those who share their stories.
- **Share Stories** (20 minutes total per person = 10 minutes for one person to share, then 10 minutes for the group to encourage the person, then one group member prays for the person). You can generally have 3–4 people share during a small group time. If you are in a married couples' group, the format and timing for sharing your story will be slightly different. Each couple will have twenty minutes to share. Each spouse should take five minutes to share

their story, themes, and patterns from before marriage. Then, the couple will have ten minutes to share together about agreed-upon themes and patterns within their marriage. Couples should share aspects of marriage they can celebrate as well as what they want to work through during *Restore*.

- **Pray** (5 minutes)—close out the group with a brief prayer time. Seek to end by the agreed upon time in order to respect everyone's time.

General Schedule for Lesson 13

- **Look Back** (15 minutes)—to discuss how God enabled them to live differently, based on God's invitation from the previous week's Read and Abide time.
- **Share Testimonies** (10–15 minutes total per person = 5–10 minutes for one person to share their testimony, then 5 minutes for the group to encourage the person, then one group member prays for the person). You can allow more time for the encouragement and prayer if each person has time to share their testimony during this last small group meeting.
- **Pray** (5 minutes)—close out the group with a brief prayer time. Seek to end by the agreed upon time in order to respect everyone's time.

LESSON 1: REFRAMING OUR REALITY THROUGH THE LENS OF THE FALL

- As they read through the lesson, participants should begin to reframe their struggles within the realities of the fall. As they begin to see and understand their struggles through this lens, they can have hope, knowing that the fall is not the end of God's story.
- Participants should also find relief as they understand the common struggles and realize that everyone struggles in similar ways. This lesson offers language for describing what people experience in their struggles but may not have had words to express.
- Be sure to clarify that the common struggles are not our core sins.

- Participants should grow in awareness and understanding of their heart struggles. They will also see how their common struggles lead to relational struggles, which ultimately impact how they love God and others.
- After reading the lesson and completing the response activities, encourage participants to fill out the storyboard (found in the very back of this book) at the end of each lesson. Encourage them to write down how God is *reframing* the way they see their lives and relationships as well as how he is *restoring* their souls. If they capture how God is at work through each lesson, they will be able to see the subtle and significant ways God is *redeeming* their story over the course of their journey.
- Read and Abide: Participants should see how the common struggles emerged in the story of the fall in Genesis 3.
- IMPORTANT: At the end of your time together, point out that participants will need to get started right away on lesson 2 rather than waiting until a few days before the next meeting. Ideally, working through lesson 2 requires a full week of reflection. Also, be aware that if your group is large you may want to spend more than one group meeting on lesson 2, so that everyone has a change to participate fully.

LESSON 2: FACING YOUR REALITY THROUGH YOUR STORY

Preparing Stories
- Ideally, participants should set aside a full week to work prayerfully through each step to remember, reflect, and recap their story prior to the group meeting.
- Participants may get overwhelmed or frustrated if they think they need to share their entire life in ten or twenty minutes. The lesson is designed to help participants narrow down which slice of their story they should share based on the prevailing or most painful theme in their current season of life.
- Remind participants that their themes are not limited to the common struggles. The examples in the lesson will reiterate this point.

- Remind participants they should not simply share their conversion story. Those in vocational ministry should not simply share their call to ministry.
- As participants reflect and share their stories, they will begin to see how God has been with them and how he has been taking what was meant for evil and using it for good (as Joseph said to his brothers in Genesis 50:20).
- Participants should seek to identify key themes in their stories that have shaped how they see and understand themselves and their relationship with God and others. They will also see how they respond to life, which may have resulted in patterns of loving and living that God may want to continue to develop or redeem.
- For those in a couple's group, the husband and wife should complete the first five steps individually, then take the necessary time to share their reflections with one another. Afterward, they should discuss and agree on the themes and patterns they'd like to work through together when they share their story. Couples may choose to focus on (1) a painful theme from one spouse's past that continues to impact the marriage, or (2) a marital struggle that involves both partners. Remember, your spouse's story is just as important as your own. Moreover, because God has made you one, your story is not just about you ("my story"), but includes your spouse so that you both should view your story together as "our story."

Sharing Stories

- Small Group Guidelines—when you gather, but before you share stories, read through the guidelines as a group (at the end of Lesson 2) by asking people to read one tip out loud as you go around the group. The guidelines help people to know how to listen to and encourage those who share their stories. After reading through the entire Guideline, ask the group if they have any questions. After answering any questions, ask the group, "Do you agree to follow these guidelines so that we can best love one another in the group?"
- Plan to give each participant ten minutes to share their story if they are in a women's or men's group. You may have to remind

participants of the time limits. You also might encourage them to start by telling their themes, but otherwise, give them freedom to tell their story their way.

- For those in a married couples' group, the format and timing for sharing their story will be slightly different. Each couple will have twenty minutes to share. Each spouse should take five minutes to share their story, themes, and patterns from *before* marriage. Then, the couple will have ten minutes to share together about agreed-upon themes and patterns *within* their marriage.

- If your group is large and need to share stories over two meetings given your allotted small group time, then you as the leader should share the first week, along with several others. The other half of the group can share the following week. Those in your group will take their cues from you as the leader in terms of openness, honesty, and tone.

- After an individual or a couple shares, give the group some time to encourage them. Then have one person close the encouragement time with prayer.

LESSON 3: KNOWING GOD AND HIS REALITY THROUGH HIS STORY

- We can be so consumed by our own stories that we forget about the more important story of God. This lesson helps participants look up and see God's bigger reality as revealed through his story.

- Make sure participants reflect on who God is and the reality that he enjoyed a full and complete life before creation as Father, Son, and Holy Spirit. Reflecting on this eternal reality expands our view of God and should lead to greater confidence and rest in God.

- Take time to address participants' questions about the Trinity. Given the limited scope of the lesson, the main goal is for participants to understand that since God is love, it is impossible for him not to love. God the Father shares his love with his Son through his Spirit, and he created us so that we might share in such love.

- It's important for participants to reflect on the never-changing reality of God's love because all of us struggle primarily with doubting his love, which impacts how we relate and respond to God and others.

- Check to see what questions participants have about the diagram of God's story. The diagram gives a perspective on life in a broken world. It helps us answer the question of why life is hard while reminding us that even though we are living in the fall, we are also living in Christ, so we have hope and help!
- Depending on their church background, spiritual warfare may be a new or misunderstood concept for some participants. Lesson 6 will address spiritual warfare in more detail.
- God's story has a number of themes, but *Restore* focuses on the primary **themes of love and communion** with God.
- Remind participants not to skip or gloss over the question dealing with **God's character** in the response activities. God's attributes are presented in a practical way that is relevant for our lives in a broken world.

LESSON 4: CREATION: GOD CREATED US FOR LOVE

- Lesson 4 continues the emphasis on God's story, but participants should be reassured that God doesn't minimize or deny our story when he invites us to look up to him and his story. In lessons 4–12, participants should keep their story and themes in mind so they can see how God's story and its themes address their reality.
- It's helpful to remind participants each week that God seeks to **reframe** how we see and understand our lives and relationships, as well as how we know him and how we relate and respond to him. God will also **restore** our souls as we draw near and abide with Christ, living more and more in his reality.
- The realities of creation help us to see and understand the power and wisdom of God's word. *Restore* seeks to help God's people grow confident in God's Word, compelling them to abide with Christ through his Word.
- The creation movement also helps participants to see they were **created purposefully out of God's good pleasure**. Too often, people can struggle with feeling like there is no rhyme or reason

to why they exist. They feel as if they don't know their purpose beyond the everyday demands of life.

- Ensure that those in your group ponder each of the three aspects of communion with God: knowing, experiencing, and imaging him (KEI). Such knowledge is too wonderful for us to comprehend fully (Psalm 139:6).

- Given that eternal life is defined as knowing God (John 17:3), give the group time to reflect on how such a perspective changes how they see and approach each moment of their days.

- Participants may struggle the most with the aspect of experiencing God since this reality can seem abstract or be a rare occurrence given how commonly Christians experience spiritual dryness or numbness.

- Imaging God may seem like an unimportant theological concept to most people, but it is deeply practical, impacting the way we live our everyday lives with God and others. Since Jesus is the perfect image of God, it makes sense that God calls us to image Christ, conforming ourselves more and more to his likeness. The two great love commandments sum up how we should image God; we must love God with our whole lives and love one another as Jesus has loved us (Matthew 22:37–40; John 13:34–35).

LESSON 5: CREATION: JESUS IS OVER ALL CREATION

- This lesson seeks to exalt Christ by expanding our understanding of his powerful activity and existence beyond his birth and death. We can see God's glory in the face of Christ as we reflect on the reality that all things were created in him, through him, and for him, and that he holds all things together (2 Corinthians 4:6; Colossians 1:16–17).

- You may need to help participants see the importance of making Jesus their reference point as opposed to their own story and struggles, other people, and the various philosophies and traditions of this world (Colossians 2:8). We can only understand who we are and what we were made for by knowing Jesus through his life, death, and resurrection (Philippians 3:8–10).

- Prompt the group to reflect on what it means that "all things were made through him and for him" (Colossians 1:16) as it relates to them and how they live their lives. This creation reality connects directly with another creation reality: that we were made in his image (Genesis 1:27). God not only wants us to live *with* him, but also to live *for* him.
- Give the group time to reflect on their story, themes, and pressing realities given the truth that Jesus is holding all things together, sustaining all things by his powerful word (Colossians 1:17; Hebrews 1:3). See question 2 in the response activities.
- **Look** at Jesus; **listen** to his words; **live** by faith as you follow him in obedience. These three verbs serve as a simple, reproducible, and helpful prompt as we live in this fallen world where we struggle to know where to look for help, who to listen to and what to listen for, and what we should do and how we should live.

LESSON 6: THE FALL: EVIL KEEPS US FROM LOVE
- This lesson seeks to reframe how we see and understand our struggles and evil's impact on our souls.
- Help participants see how sin's presence, promises, and power seek to counteract God's presence, promises, and power.
- Evil keeps us from love by defiling our hearts with the beat of self-love and self-glory. As a result, we actively and passively respond to evil's presence, promises, and power with common struggles, relational struggles, and faith struggles. These struggles feed off of one another and are always present as we live in the fall, even though we live in Christ.
- Help participants see how they personally experience the schemes of the Enemy—deception, distraction, discouragement, and division. Ensure they see how the Enemy's tactics impact how they relate and respond to God, others, and themselves.
- Help participants see how they personally experience faith struggles—doubts, despair, and distance. Ensure they see how such struggles impact their relationship with God, others, and themselves.

- Participants will be on a spectrum regarding anger with God. Some are not aware of their anger with God. Others are aware, but they may not want to acknowledge it. Still others openly express such anger.
- Give participants time to reflect on their doubts, or unbelief, toward God. Even though our doubts are common, they are not harmless. In fact, they damage our soul and harm our relationship with God and others. Without the "shield of faith," we are defenseless against the fiery arrows of the enemy (Ephesians 6:16).
- As participants become aware of what drives their faith struggles, and even their anger with God, they will understand how God invites them to reframe the way they see him and his relationship with them.
- Ensure that participants don't leave defeated after this lesson. Remind them that the fall is not the end of God's story.

LESSON 7: THE FALL: TEMPTATION, SIN, AND BROKEN RELATIONSHIPS

- The story of David helps us understand the nature of temptation, godly sorrow, confession, and repentance. Unfortunately, confession of sin is often equated with repentance. As a result, people confess their sins and end up merely empathizing with one another, accepting their sins as a way of life. Help participants understand that confession is just a start and should lead to a full repentance, turning away from sin and turning to and trusting Christ through obedience.
- God's people can become discouraged and lose heart in the midst of ongoing temptation to sin. Remind them that the enemy wants to use the temptations, which are meant for evil, to draw them away from Christ. Yet God takes what is meant for evil and uses it for good (Genesis 50:20). Encourage the group to use their temptations as a trigger, or prompt, to remind them to run to Jesus for refuge and hope. Temptations should remind us of our desperate need for Jesus, which in turn makes us humbler and more dependent upon Jesus.

- Help people to reframe their broken relationships within the impact of the fall. The good news is that Jesus Christ came to reconcile the most important relationship that has been broken by evil—his own relationship with his people. Reframing our broken relationships within the reality of God's story reminds us that God calls us to reconcile our broken relationships with others the same way Jesus Christ reconciled his broken relationship with us—through love and forgiveness.
- Psalm 51 (Read and Abide) serves as a helpful guide for confession and repentance, and it functions as a needed corrective to common problems with our confession and repentance.

Reflect and Pray: Steps for Reconciling a Broken Relationship

- Encourage participants to read through this section (outside of the group time) even if they don't think they have any broken relationships. As they work through the six steps, the Spirit of God will help them see who they may need to pursue with love, or love by forgiving.
- Each step is important and intentional. Note the goals for each step.
- Encourage participants to pay particular attention to the steps involved in confessing to others. We typically say we are sorry for how we hurt someone, but we rarely ask them to share how we have hurt them. Another mistake is that we may apologize but not end the confession by asking for forgiveness.
- Even though a relationship is reconciled when both parties confess, ask for, and offer forgiveness, it may take time to restore the relationship, which requires rebuilding trust and commitment.

LESSON 8: JESUS RESTORES US WITH LOVE

- God's story not only reframes how we see and understand our lives and relationships, but also reminds us that Jesus came to restore our souls.
- This lesson helps us understand the extraordinary sufferings of Christ as he lived and died in order to restore us with love.

- First, help participants to see that Jesus, as our perfect high priest, experienced immeasurably more temptation, injustice, oppression, abuse, betrayal, and abandonment than we could ever face in this broken world (Hebrews 2:17–18). Second, ensure they connect how Jesus's sufferings enable him to be fully aware of our struggles and to understand the care we need in our times of trouble.
- As we follow Jesus, we can endure the trials of life like Jesus did with hope and help, knowing that our Good Shepherd is with us as we journey through the dark valleys of life.
- We not only learn obedience through suffering as Jesus did, but we also come to know the heights and depths of his love as we seek refuge in him.

LESSON 9: REDEMPTION: WE LIVE IN GOD'S PRESENCE

- Ensure that participants reflect on the four stated reasons why God is confident in his salvation work and we can't mess it up. Ask how these redemption realities make a difference in how they see and understand their lives and relationships in this broken world.
- God knows we can struggle with feeling alone and not belonging, given the difficulties of relationships in a fallen world. A major theme in God's story is the reality that *God is with us*. God ensures the reality of his never-ending presence by placing his people in union with Christ through his indwelling Spirit (Romans 8:9–11).
- We can be underwhelmed by the reality that we are always living in God's presence while being overwhelmed by life. We can trivialize the remarkable reality of living in Christ by pretending that "Jesus is sitting next to me in an empty chair" or "he is in the front seat with me." If some in your group struggle with being underwhelmed with the reality of living in God's presence, take time to pray and ask God to help their unbelief (Mark 9:24). God's Spirit can also overwhelm them as they read and abide through Psalm 84.
- Be sure to work through and discuss the three benefits of living in God's presence outlined in the response activities. Afterwards,

reflect on how you can live differently in God's story given your union with Christ.

LESSON 10: REDEMPTION: WE LIVE IN GOD'S PROMISES

- God knows we can struggle with trust, whether it's trusting him or others. Everywhere we turn, someone or something is letting us down. When life takes unexpected turns, we can wrongly believe that God has broken his promises to us.
- A major theme in God's story is trust, or faith, in God. The enemy seeks to weaken our faith in God by leveraging the troubles in our life to undermine our confidence in who God is, and to convince us that God doesn't have the power to do what he promised.
- Our trust in God centers on the Word of God. Are his words true? Will he do what he promised? When we doubt God's Word, we doubt everything about God including his character and his promises. The Spirit empowers us to trust that all of God's promises are yes and guaranteed in Christ (2 Corinthians 1:20).
- Because of our union with Christ, we are always living in God's promises, which are true for every one of God's people, all of the time, no exception.
- Out of the three promises of God highlighted in the lesson, it will be interesting to see how different people will struggle differently to believe or receive a certain promise based on what they have experienced in their story.
- The response activities will help participants see how the broken promises of others in their story, in addition to the relentless spiritual warfare which seeks to fill them with unbelief, impact how they lack trust in the guaranteed promises of God.

LESSON 11: REDEMPTION: WE LIVE IN GOD'S POWER

- God knows that we struggle with being weak and broken, and that this can lead to living powerless lives. When we see ourselves as helpless, we can become cynical and settle for just surviving. In our discouragement and despair, we can turn our backs on God, convinced that Jesus doesn't make a difference in our lives. In the worst cases, we can conclude that life is not worth living.

- Encourage the group to reflect on 2 Peter 1:3–4, which declares that God's **presence** and **promises** are guaranteed through God's **power** that has been given to us. Again, we can be underwhelmed by the reality of living in God's power even though it's the same power that raised Christ from the dead (Ephesians 1:19–21).

- Each section of this lesson is meant to deepen your **confidence** in God and your **conviction** that he has the power to do what he promised—to guard your heart with his peace and to restore your soul (Philippians 4:6–7; Psalm 23:3). As God enlarges your shield of faith, you will be able to endure life's relentless storms with more hope, even joy.

- Hopefully, by this part of the journey, everyone in the group should already be aware of their weakness and their powerlessness against evil, and willing to acknowledge it. If there are some who still claim to be strong, you can expect to see weariness in them as they try to fight in their own strength, and exhaustion as they seek to control their lives and everything around them.

- We will bear fruit as God's Spirit empowers us to live a desperate and dependent life with Christ. We can be confident that, as we follow Christ on his paths of righteousness, we will taste and experience more and more of the fruit of the Spirit (Galatians 5:22–23).

LESSON 12: CONSUMMATION: WE WILL ENJOY LOVE FOREVER

- For most of us, anticipating the future reality of the new heaven and earth gives momentary relief, but the pain and heartache cries for more immediate help and relief.

- When we realize God is the common denominator between our present reality and our future hope, we can find immediate rest, knowing that (1) the God who will wipe away every tear and take away all pain and death is the same God who comforts us now in all of our troubles, and (2) we can partially enjoy now what we will one day enjoy fully: God himself and his glorious love. Because of our union with Christ, we can experience the joy and pleasure of Christ even in the midst of our brokenness.

- Creation and consummation serve as bookends that inform how we should live now, in between how God first created us to live and how we will live forever.
- Encourage the group members to look back through their journaling activity (Look Back section) in Lesson 1 and their Storyboard.

LESSON 13: REFLECTION, NEXT STEPS, AND TESTIMONY

- This last lesson gives the participants the chance to reflect on how they have seen God reframe how they see all of life, how God has been restoring their souls, and redeeming their stories.
- The table in the "Reflection" section is designed to help people to compare their understanding and experiences before and after *Restore*. The journaling activity in Lesson 1, their storyboard, and their before and after reflections in this table will help them to develop their testimony.
- Encourage the group to prayerfully consider the next steps God is inviting them to take given their journey through God's story. Encourage them to consider next steps from the standpoint of both a disciple and a disciple maker.
- During this meeting, take time to share testimonies based on the guidelines in the reading. As each person shares, the others in the group should be encouraged to offer additional ways they have seen God at work in the life of the participant who just shared. Take time to pray for one another after each participant shares and is encouraged.

MY STORYBOARD

MY THEMES AT THE START OF *RESTORE* (FROM LESSON 2)

Reframe	Restore
Here are ways God is *reframing* how I see my life and my struggles, how I see him, and how I see others.	Here are ways God is *restoring* my soul. (You might use the fruit of the Spirit in Galatians 5:22–23, the Spirit-dependent goals from "How to Use This Workbook," and "What It Means for Jesus to Restore Our Souls" in Lesson 13 as prompts for how God is restoring your soul.)

Lesson 1
Reframing Our
Reality Through
the Lens of the
Fall

Lesson 3
Knowing God
and His Reality
Through His
Story

Reframe	Restore

Lesson 4
Creation: God
Created Us for
Love

Lesson 5
Creation: Jesus
Is Over All
Creation

Lesson 6
The Fall: Evil
Keeps Us from
Love

Lesson 7
The Fall:
Temptation,
Sin, and Broken
Relationships

**Reconciling
a Broken
Relationship**

Reframe	Restore

Lesson 8
Redemption:
Jesus Restores
Us with Love

Lesson 9
Redemption: We
Live in God's
Presence

Lesson 10
Redemption: We
Live in God's
Promises

Lesson 11
Redemption: We
Live in God's
Power

Lesson 12
Consummation:
We Will Enjoy
Love Forever

REDEEM

HERE ARE WAYS GOD IS *REDEEMING* MY STORY

ENDNOTES

1. The distinction between encouragement and affirmation comes from Judy Dabler, Creative Conciliation, http://www.creativeconciliation.org

2. Michael Reeves, *Delighting in the Trinity* (Downers Grove, IL: InterVarsity, 2012), 26.

3. Richard R. Melick, Jr., *The New American Commentary: Philippians, Colossians, Philemon* (Nashville, TN: Broadman Press), 217.

4. For additional resources on this topic, I recommend *If God is Good* by Randy Alcorn, *Suffering* by Paul David Tripp, *When God Weeps* by Joni Eareckson Tada, and *Suffering and the Heart of God* by Diane Langberg. To approach this topic with children, I recommend *The Moon is Always Round* by Jonathan Gibson.

5. Powlison, *Good and* Angry, 39–41.

6. Robert Bergin, *The New American Commentary: 1, 2 Samuel* (Nashville, TN: B&H Publishing, 1996), 364.

7. This understanding of worldly sorrow is adapted from Charles Hodge, *1 & 2 Corinthians* (Edinburgh: Banner of Truth, 1974) and from Philip E. Hughes, *The Second Epistle to the Corinthians* (Grand Rapids, MI: Eerdmans, 1962).

8. This multi-step confession process adapted from Judy Dabler, Creative Conciliation, http://www.creativeconciliation.org.

9. Charles Spurgeon, *Spurgeon's Expository Encyclopedia* (Grand Rapids, MI: Baker, 1996), 321.

10. John Piper, "Why Did Jesus Cry, 'My God, My God, Why Have You Forsaken Me?'" Desiring God website, March 1, 2016, www.desiringgod.org/interviews/my-god-my-god-why-have-you-forsaken-me-didnt-jesus-already-know.

RESTORE

GOSPEL CARE MINISTRIES

Gospel Care Ministries
helps leaders and churches
to be confident in Christ as
they live and serve in the
brokenness of life.

To learn more about using Restore as a church
ministry to build a culture of discipleship and
care in community, go to

www.gospel.care